Beyond Resilience

Trench-Tested Tools to Thrive Under Pressure

Dan Diamond, MD

NogginStorm, LLC
9188 Utah ST NE
Bremerton, WA 98311
www.dandiamondmd.com

Cover Design: **Dyanne Cavero**

Beyond Resilience: Trench-Tested Tools to Thrive Under Pressure / Dan Diamond, MD. -- 1st ed.
ISBN 978-0-9970594-0-3

*Dedicated to Dr. Jullette Saussy
and the Heroes of
The New Orleans Emergency Medical Services*

*"True heroism is remarkably sober, very
undramatic. It is not the urge to surpass all others
at whatever cost, but the urge to serve others at
whatever cost."*

—ARTHUR ASHE

Contents

The Problem

*"A hospital bed is a parked taxi with
the meter running."*

Groucho Marx

Health Care is a Risky Business

No doubt, we are in the midst of the greatest change in the history of health care, and it is coming at an ever increasing pace. Reimbursements continue to decline while the cost of delivering care increases due to aging of the population, increasing government regulation, and the expanding infrastructure required to meet the need. According to a survey commissioned by the Physicians Foundation in 2012, six out of ten physicians said that they would quit medicine if they could. Unfortunately, physicians are not alone. In a 2011 American Nurses Association survey, 74% of nurses said that their greatest workplace hazard was the effects of stress and being overworked. Estimates place the cost of workplace turnover at twice the salary of the physician or nurse.

The increased demand for services by patients seeking health care services as a result of the Affordable Care Act (ACA), combined with the demands of "meaningful use" of the electronic medical record

(EMR), decrease the amount of time that providers can spend with patients. This in turn impacts patient satisfaction surveys that are tied to reimbursement. It takes time to be kind, and right now most health care professionals no longer have enough time to go above and beyond. Despite the fact that more patients now have insurance coverage than ever before, the situation is not necessarily any better for the average patient. The insurance companies have simply shifted more costs to the patient. More patients are now enrolled with high deductible programs or programs with increased co-pay fees. Patients feel the brunt of this and often times put off getting care until problems become more complex. This can result in much more complicated patients that need to be seen in a system that is already overloaded and trying to improve efficiencies. Front-line health care workers are forced to prioritize problems for patients and do the best they can to address the issues in the short amount of time that is allotted.

The new system also shifts the financial burden to the health care providers and institutions as they too try to collect the high deductible debts. Unfortunately, this can lead to a higher amount of unpaid fees, which in turn leads to tighter budgets, decreased staffing and increased stress for those that are caring for the patients and those that are managing departments. It is a complicated problem.

Survival of the Fittest or Survival of the Fastest?

Major metropolitan areas are now developing centers of excellence in order to deliver efficient and cost-effective care. Community hospitals will have a difficult time competing for the same health care dollars. They also face the challenge of decreased access to capital. Many hospitals are wrestling with the question of whether or not they are going to be able to continue to provide services in their community. Strategic alliances become more and more important.

As acquisitions become more commonplace, many staff members wonder whether or not they are going to continue to have a job. And, if they continue to have a job, will it still be rewarding? Will they get paid enough to pay their own bills? As our health care expenditures consume a greater amount of the gross national product every year, eventually we are going to have to face the questions of whether or not we are going to ration care. The United States is the only developed country that does not have a health care budget. That will not last for long. These changes are not optional; they are coming – like it or not.

The Uncertain Future of Health Care

These are times of outrageous change. The old metrics of "butts in the bed" is a thing of the past. In other words, hospitals used to make their money based on what they did. We are now shifting to a time of population health management. That sounds like Ivory Tower speak but the impact is enormous. Hospitals will no longer be the central hub of the health care system. Full stop. Think about the consequences of that! If the hospital is not the central hub, then who will be? Who will be responsible for the health care of our communities? The system will reward organizations that keep people healthy and out of the hospital. The central hub will soon become health care companies that will focus on managing the health of the population. It is likely that today is the best revenue that hospitals will see over the next 10 years.

Consider the consequences for you personally if today is as good as it gets. How will your job be impacted? What will your job look like next year? Hospitals have already absorbed $122 billion in new cuts since 2010. We are now moving into the "retailization" of health care. The new health care companies do not want patients, they want customers. This is not a subtle shift. This is a philosophical shift with huge implications for those of us on the frontlines. We already "say" that we work for the patient... but soon we actually will. They will have more choices than ever before, and some of those choices are going to significantly impact the financial stability of the organizations that we work for now.

As of 2014, CVS pharmacies had 836 Minute Clinics and Walgreens had 388. Using Theranos labs, Walgreens is now charging patients $7.27 for a comprehensive metabolic panel, while the average cost in the US is currently $30 with some institutions charging as much as $135. Patients will love it because it only takes a single drop of blood. How will this change patient behavior? Will they still have outpatient labs drawn at your facility? Who will input the lab results into your EMR if they are done at CVS or Walgreens? How will this impact the viability of your lab? How would your job change if you did not have the powerful lab that you have now? If you work in a clinic, will you have a lab? Will patients come to see you or will they go somewhere where they can get their labs drawn at one third the cost?

Half of the adults in the US belong to Walgreens Balance Rewards Loyalty Program. If you know what a patient's health care habits are, you can control and direct their behavior. Walgreens already knows who 50% of the diabetics in the US are. They know their name, address, email, phone and spending habits. With that sort of information and insights, it is possible to impact patient behavior through targeted campaigns. How will hospitals and health care organizations compete? How will hospitals survive if they lose their profit centers of lab and imaging?

Medicine is the greatest driver of the ever increasing US national debt. Our nation cannot and will not be able to afford to pay for health care as it is currently being delivered. We will simply run out of money.

So how will these tectonic changes impact your work? If you are on the frontlines taking care of patients, will you still have a hospital to work in if the lab is no longer a profit center that offsets the cost of the care you are delivering? How will the hospitals cover the costs of readmissions which have no reimbursement like congestive heart failure? How will they cut back further? Fewer nurses? Fewer doctors? Longer shifts? How will they handle patient surges? Will there be more per diem staff and more traveling nurses? What about your own health insurance? Will the hospitals still be able to pay for your benefits? Will they shift you to a higher and higher deductible?

If you are trying to manage a department, how will you address the shifting expectations? How will these changes impact your staffing and your budget? Will departments like respiratory therapy survive or will their duties be shifted to the nursing staff? How will these changes impact patient: staff ratios? Did I mention morale? Burnout? Staff retention? Recruitment?

We are heading for some challenging times indeed.

Trench-tested Tools to Thrive Under Pressure

You do not need an earthquake to have a disaster. Clearly, health care is on shaky ground. Some staff members, teams, and even entire hospitals will not make it.

However, in the midst of these challenging times, some will actually thrive.

We are not the first sector to undergo dramatic change. There are plenty of examples of radical change. When this happens some people crumple and become defeated while others excel. Some cling on to the status quo like a drowning man holds onto his gold. The transportation industry, for example, is clearly in a state of change. Uber took advantage of an industry that was not meeting the needs of the public and provided what the people wanted. As a result, Uber radically changed the world for taxi drivers and taxi companies. In fact, Uber is about to impact the health care world as well. They are now starting to offer house calls! Uber will deliver a nurse practitioner or physician to you wherever you are. Talk about giving patients what they want! The world of health care is shifting but patients still need care. Who is going to deliver it? Walgreens? Clinics? Hospitals? Outpatient centers? Change does not mean disaster for everyone. The health care industry is not going to disappear. The question is, are you going to be a part of it and are you going to come out on top?

In 1975, Salvador Maddi led a 12-year study of over 450 male and female supervisors, managers and decision makers at Illinois Bell Telephone. When the U.S. Federal Court ordered the massive deregulation of the "Ma Bell" monopoly, it resulted in a loss of 12,000 jobs by the end of 1982. Two thirds of the employees that lost their jobs broke down and succumbed to health issues such as depression, anxiety, alcoholism or heart disease. However, one third excelled and actually ended up better off than they were before the deregulation. Maddi described three keys that differentiated those that did well: commitment, control and challenge. Those that excelled stayed committed to the process. They believed that they could control their future and they approached the transition as a challenge.

In response to the drastic changes in health care, there has been an increasing emphasis on resilience. Resilience is defined as:

1. The ability of a substance or object to spring back into shape; elasticity.
2. The capacity to recover quickly from difficulties; toughness.

But, resilience is no longer enough. It is not enough to "spring back into shape" because the shape of our current health care is not meeting the need. It is no longer enough to "recover quickly". We need a new strategy. It is not enough to just survive. We need to think differently. This is a time of tremendous opportunity for the individuals and organizations that can adapt, engage and innovate.

Urgent or Emergent: There is No Time to Lose

In 2014, more rural hospitals closed in the US than in the prior 15 years combined. More physicians, nurses and administrators are feeling burned out and overwhelmed. However, the challenges we face are going to accelerate and become even more significant. Our health care system needs fully engaged people that are equipped with trench-tested tools to shape the future of health care. We need strong teams and we need the junctions between teams to be stronger than ever. If you value job security, it is no longer going to be enough to try to figure out how to protect your turf. We no longer have time for that.

The most valuable people in your organization are going to be those that can see beyond their own team. Again, consider how long it took for the taxi industry to change. I am sure that for the individual cab drivers, the change seemed to happen overnight. One day they were busy and the next day they had plenty of time to sit in their cabs and wonder what just happened. Health care is moving just as fast, but we can see these changes coming. As the delivery of health care becomes more commercialized (or retail-ized) it will bring a whole new aggressive and innovative leadership force to the table. Our existing health care team needs to stand up and get involved, or the other forces involved will determine the direction of care while we just sit there waiting for the next patient to show up.

Disasters and the Unstoppables

Serving as the Director of the Medical Triage Unit at the New Orleans Convention Center after Hurricane Katrina was one of the most intense experiences of my life. It was surreal. One day I am seeing patients in my clinic and the next day I am running the only functioning medical facility in the entire city of New Orleans. I had intense dreams for a month after I came home. My perspective was altered and my eyes were opened. I saw human motivation and behavior with a newfound clarity. When all of the external "show" is stripped from people's lives it is easy to see their mindset and strategies. The playing field was leveled. Everyone was without their resources. We were all street people.

Despite responding to international disasters around the globe, what I experienced in New Orleans following Katrina radically changed my perspective. I expected to see victims. The military was standing by with 50,000 body bags. We knew this was going to be a bad one. However, there was something that got my attention and piqued my curiosity. I was inspired by the people that, despite losing everything, did NOT become victims. I came home wanting to understand why and how some people become unstoppable.

When we look at those that have overcome tremendous odds, it can make us a bit uncomfortable. I found myself asking hard questions like, "If those people can do so much despite losing everything, why am I not making more of a difference with my life in the midst of my abundance?" It is those difficult questions at the interface between good and great that challenge us to rise to the occasion and leave a legacy.

This book is a product of wrestling with those questions. My heart's desire is to equip you to make a difference as you face the challenge of delivering world-class health care. Which way will you face? Will you look at and identify with those that become victims or will you be challenged and compelled by those that overcome. This book will reveal the secrets of those that are unstoppable. Applying them to your life will change you, empower you and impact those you serve.

Dana's Story

Years ago my medical assistant was on the verge of losing her job. Dana had already been "written up" a couple of times. Her heart wasn't in her work and it showed. She had taken on the mindset of a victim. Everyone on the team knew it. She was sucking the energy out of our group. Her negativity was contagious. On one occasion we had a particularly difficult day. There was one physician in our group that everyone tried to figure out when he was going to go on vacation because every time he left, we were slammed with phone calls. He was one of those folks that couldn't say "no" to anyone. Consequently, every patient for a hundred miles that wanted a prescription for controlled substances came to him. When he was on vacation, those of us that took his calls were inundated with requests for medications that we didn't want to fill. This was before the days of electronic medical records so we didn't even have access to his charts since his office was in another town. But still the calls came and we had to deal with it. I always figured that I would retire the week before he did.

Then everything changed one day. He left the clinic. We all had to scramble to deal with the patients and their less than reasonable demands. We were on call just days after he left and by 10 AM my medical assistant lost it. She pitched a full blown tantrum including pounding her fists on the table as she was yelling, "You have to DO SOMETHING! I can't get my work done! I can't even take our own calls! We don't have access to

17

his charts! This just isn't working. I can't do it!" I can still see and hear her in my brain. I let her rant for a bit because honestly, I agreed with her.

When she calmed down I told her about the research that I was doing about the mindsets of victims and thrivers and I took a piece of paper out and jotted down some of the core principles in this book. It was a simple drawing. Great principles that have changed my life are always simple. It took me months of work to boil the concepts down to a simple but memorable format. I handed her the paper and went in to see my next patient.

When I emerged from the exam room a short while later, she was gone. The "victim" that is. Dana was there but she was a completely new person. She was excited, she had passion and she was out to change the world! It was, to be frank, shocking. I stood there with my jaw on the ground as she shared her plan with me. She realized that there was a way to fix the situation. Since we had someone extra in training working with us, she figured that we could send one of our staff to the other clinic where they would have access to the charts. That person could then use my protocols and take care of the refills. They would only have to call if they had a question. The staff at the other office would be able to have a "normal" day without the stress of all of the overwhelming requests to answer all of our questions about the patients and when their last refill was. It was a tremendous idea. I immediately got on the phone and told our clinic's Medical Director about it. He was excited. The other clinic was ecstatic! "You would do that for us? Really? Wow! You guys are great!"

> She had gone from a powerless, self-absorbed victim to an empowered person that changed our world by putting the needs of others first. It was dramatic. Not only did she save her job, she went on to become one of our best employees...of all time. Several months later, as we were implementing our new electronic medical record system, she was the cheerleader that inspired all of us. I'll always remember overhearing her say to the staff, "Come on you guys, we have the power to choose how we are going to respond and it's not all about us. It's about delivering outstanding care to our patients!"

If you are a manager or director, what's that worth to you? If you're on the front-lines, how would this type of shift impact your job satisfaction or even the likelihood of keeping your job when the layoffs come?

This book is about that sort of transformation. It is about the nuts and bolts of adopting the Thriver's Mindset and going on to change your world. It is about rediscovering your defining purpose, guarding your passion and learning to problem solve and move forward despite tremendous pressure. These concepts are not just some lofty ideas from the Ivory Tower; these are trench-tested principles that were forged in the depths of some of the world's greatest disasters. These tools will change your life and change your world.

It is human nature to cry out at some point, "How in the world am I going to survive?" But surviving is no longer enough. I will never forget watching the Seattle Seahawks kicking a punt to the St Louis Rams during their December 2013 game. Justin Veltung of the Rams

19

struggled to keep his balance as he back peddled to catch the ball. He was absolutely flattened by the fast moving man with momentum, Ricardo Lockette. Just trying to catch the ball is not enough; we have to lean in and drive ahead. Those that only try to figure out how they will just survive will find themselves flat on their backs. We need to meet our challenges with momentum, creativity and enthusiasm. In order to come through these challenging times of change and leave a legacy, we need to move beyond resilience and focus on **performance** under pressure. Just like an Olympic physician that helps athletes perform at their peak, my goal is not to just help you survive; my goal is to help you thrive.

This book will equip you to turn:

- confusion into clarity
- adversity into opportunity
- pressure into productivity
- and the indescribable mess of disaster into solutions

Part I: Target Fixation

*"You have brains in your head.
You have feet in your shoes.
You can steer yourself in any direction
you choose.
You're on your own, and you know
what you know.
And you are the guy who'll decide
where to go."*

Dr. Seuss

Devil's Gulch

In the mountains surrounding Wenatchee, WA there is an amazing mountain bike trail appropriately named Devil's Gulch. It is a 24-mile descent with a 3000ft drop. It is all single track and there are some places where the trail is less than 2ft wide. On the wrong side of the trail, in places, there are drop offs that exceed a hundred feet or more. If a rider loses concentration for even a second, the consequences can be disastrous...even deadly.

We took turns being the lead rider. It was a real adrenaline rush with plenty of twists and turns. I'm not one for heights so I was a bit nervous as we flew down the hill. And then it happened. Just for a second — and I do mean just a second — I took my eyes off the center of the trail and looked to the right at the drop off. Just as I was thinking that I needed to be careful and not fall off the cliff, my bike launched off the edge.

I was the lead bike and a long way ahead of the guy behind me. As I was going over the edge I thought, "They will never even know where I went!" Fortunately, about 10-15 feet down there was a clump of shrubbery sticking out and I landed in that. It wasn't a graceful landing but I was certainly grateful for something to keep me from going all the way down. The first few bikers went streaking by but the fourth guy heard me yelling for help. As I passed my bike up to the guys above and scrambled back up to the trail, I realized that I had just experienced the Law of Target Fixation: "You go where you look".

This is a critical concept when facing a rapidly changing and threatening environment. If I start my day out coming up with three reason why I do not like my job, by the end of the day I will have five reasons. If I start my day out saying that I *like* my job for the following three reasons, by the end of the day I will come up with five reasons why I *like* my job. Think about your relationship with your significant other. The list that you keep will have a dramatic impact on your overall relationship. After more than 30 years of marriage, I have proven this to be true. The list that I focus on is the one that grows. I have a choice: focus on what I like about my wife or what drives me crazy. Either way, the list I focus on will grow by the end of the day. I go where I look. The variable is not my wife.

Where we look is also contagious to other people. Think about the last time you passed somebody on the street and they were looking up in the air. You could not help but glance to see where they were looking. The same thing happens in the workplace. It is all too easy to get sucked into negativity. On the contrary, if you keep your gaze locked in the direction that you want to go or in the direction you want to move your team, you are much more likely to succeed.

Remember the donkey in Winnie the Pooh? Eeyore was famous for growing his negative list. Sauntering along he mumbles, "It always rains on my birthday but what's the use, no one remembers anyway." With all of the mergers and acquisitions that are happening in heath care, whether you are on the front lines or in management, it is easy to keep your own Eeyore's list. It could be something like this (yes, this is a list of my own that I have had to deal with):

1. They are going to change us to a new EMR.
2. They are going to change our formulary and we cannot use the medications that we are convinced are the best.
3. Bulk purchasing power is great but they are making us use stuff that is cheap and doesn't work as well as the stuff we had before.
4. Decisions are being made in a completely different state or maybe a different planet altogether! There's no way I can have a say in what happens around here.
5. No one cares about my perspective or ideas.

If you read this list with Eeyore's voice in your head, you can even start to feel the heaviness of the list. If I ponder my Eeyore's list, it really does not take much effort to grow it. In the process of growing it, invariably I become more discouraged and feel compelled to share my frustrations with others. Soon, they are being impacted vicariously by my Eeyore's list. They simply grab my list and tack it onto the end of theirs. Eeyore's lists are more contagious than norovirus on a cruise ship.

However, the opposite can also be true. Imagine the impact if I start my day quoting a list like this:

1. We now have an opportunity to improve patient care by studying best practices throughout this large organization. We do not have to reinvent the wheel.

2. Because of our size, we can now negotiate better contracts with insurance companies or Accountable Care Organizations (ACOs) and avoid some of the budget cuts.

3. If I have a great idea, it is possible that it may impact the lives of patients and staff throughout the entire organization.

4. We have resources to try new pilot projects that could redefine the standard of care.

5. We have a louder political voice that can have a national impact.

Clearly, we go where we look. In the Devil's Gulch story, I was the only one that shot off the cliff because the guy behind me could not see me. In the workplace it is much easier to impact a lot of people. Attitudes and vision are both very contagious. Not only do we go where we look, others go there as well. Be vigilant and beware of Eeyore and his lists. When you hear him start to list his woes, use it as a springboard to refocus on where you actually want to go. The impact of this subtle shift is enormous. While you're at it, you will inevitably take others with you as well.

Engagement is Critical

2% of the revenues that hospitals receive from the federal government are linked to patient satisfaction and outcomes. That may not seem like much, but the average margin for a hospital is now only 3-4%. Take away the patient satisfaction and outcome dollars and that could easily be enough to shut the doors on many of the hospitals in the US. Both satisfaction and outcomes have been shown to be directly impacted by the level of employee engagement. A lack of employee engagement can cost a hospital millions of dollars in lost federal income. This in turn impacts each department and the people that work there. When the budget money dries up, the cuts become inevitable. As we transition from a fee-for-service health care model to a fee-for-performance model, patient satisfaction and outcomes will become even more essential for financial performance and viability.

In addition, employee engagement has a direct impact on employee retention. With increasing shortages for physicians and nurses this can become increasingly costly as well. There are two ways to look at this. If you're a department director, you're looking at how you can stay within your budget. Every time you lose an employee, it costs you at least double their annual salary to replace them.

If we look at this from the perspective of being an employee, we are more likely to improve our job satisfaction, become eligible for promotions and discover meaning in our work when we are engaged. Simply put, it is much more enjoyable to work at a job where we feel like we are able to make a positive difference in the lives of others.

Face Success: You Go Where You Look

(Please see the Appendix to view the complete model: Face Success: You Go Where You Look)

Actively Disengaged

> *"If I had to choose the form of betrayal that emerged most frequently from my research and that was the most dangerous in terms of corroding the trust connection, I would say disengagement."*
>
> *Brené Brown*

My medical assistant, Dana, was actively disengaged and she was bringing down the entire team. According to a Towers Watson survey done in 2007 – 2008, 3% of the US health care workforce is Actively Disengaged. When considering the impact of engagement, it is important to consider both the internal impact within the employee as well as the external impact on the team, the organization and the patients.

Internal Impact of the Actively Disengaged

Actively disengaged employees tend to become self focused. Anger can become their predominant emotion and they tend to have catastrophic reactions to challenges. They say things like, "We NEVER have enough staff!" or "I ALWAYS get the difficult patients!" Their focus on the negative, infused with anger, eats away at them from the inside out. They are not only not helping you, they are hurting you. Their anger tends to motivate them to try to recruit others and that contributes to their external impact.

External Impact of the Actively Disengaged

Actively disengaged employees discourage teams by redirecting focus on to the negative aspects of their job. The impact of target fixation can magnify problems and rapidly derail teams. They sabotage the efforts of leaders and other team members. Their caustic, contagious criticisms spread like wildfire and build division rapidly. Patients feel the impact of these folks and describe them as "grumpy" or downright "angry". They are like a virus that infects its host and rapidly depletes the host resources. Unchecked, they can be fatal.

Passively Disconnected

"Highly engaged employees make the customer experience. Disengaged employees break it."

Timothy R. Clark

The Towers Watson study found that 19% of the US health care workforce is "Disenchanted". In other words, they have become Passively Disconnected. They are not actively sabotaging, but their impact can be felt throughout the organization nonetheless because they consume resources rather than contributing to the success of the organization.

Internal Impact of the Passively Disconnected

Passively disconnected employees have a pessimistic outlook on life. They see themselves as helpless. In the chapter on the Victim Mindset, we will explore the concept of helplessness in much greater detail. Because Passively Disconnected people feel helpless and pessimistic they tend to consume their time focusing on irrelevant tasks. They clock in and clock out, but do not leave an impact. They consume resources because they focus on their perception that their needs are not being met. They expect someone to take care of them.

External Impact of the Passively Disconnected

Passively disconnected people frustrate teams because they focus on irrelevant tasks and do not help the team move forward. They start tasks but do not finish them. They drain the team's energy. Because they lead to increasing frustration and depleted energy their passive disconnectivity can become quite contagious. It begins subtle enough but the impact can become profound. As they pull their team down, some people will actually move past them to become Actively Disengaged.

Passively Connected

> *"Experience is not worth the getting.*
> *It's not a thing that happens*
> *pleasantly to a passive you – it's a*
> *wall that an active you runs up*
> *against."*
>
> *F. Scott Fitzgerald*

According to the same Towers Watson study, 44% of the health care workforce is "Enrolled". They are passively connected. They contribute to the overall success of the organization, but their impact is blunted by their lack of engagement. There is a significant difference between the Passively Disconnected people and the Passively Connected people. That difference has to do with the direction they face. Actively disengaged and passively disconnected people face towards the negative and therefore (due to the law of Target Fixation) actually move in that direction. Passively Connected and Actively Engaged people head in the opposite direction along the spectrum. They head towards success.

Internal Impact of the Passively Connected

Passively connected people are followers. They tend to be task focused and unaware of the big picture. They still consume time and energy because they wait to be told what to do, but they are headed in the right direction. This group of folks tends to be overlooked when it comes to potential. They do not stick out in a negative sense because they do not cause trouble and they do what they are told, but they also do not stick out positively. It is a subtle shift to move them to being Actively Engaged, but the consequences can be magnificent. Moving them from being "satisfied" with their job to being "energized" by their job impacts the whole team.

External Impact of the Passively Connected

Although Passively Connected people are moving in the right direction, they still stifle teamwork because they do not see the picture beyond themselves. Their world is limited to the tasks that they been assigned. They require constant direction and either are afraid to take action on their own or do not see the opportunity to do so. Because they do not actively contribute without direction, they slow creativity for the team. They wait for others to tell them what to do rather than looking for opportunities to improve the team's impact.

Actively Engaged

> *"I have learned a deep respect for one of Goethe's couplets: Whatever you can do or dream you can, begin it. Boldness has genius, power, and magic in it. Begin it now."*
>
> *Josh Leibner*

Actively Engaged people can be summed up with one powerful word: ownership. Not only do they own the success of their work, but they own the success of their team and the success of the organization. They go above and beyond. Actively Engaged people inspire others to contribute. They are exceedingly valuable.

31

Internal Impact of the Actively Engaged

Internally, Actively Engaged people see the big picture. They move beyond being task focused and have become solution focused. They are compelled by their ownership mentality. They look for opportunities constantly to improve themselves, their team and the organization. They have an internal energy that they use to take initiative. Because they are solution focused, they are more likely to overcome discouragement and stay engaged under pressure. Deep within, they are driven by the *Why* of what they are doing rather than *What* they are doing.

External Impact of the Actively Engaged

Actively Engaged people adapt readily to change and inspire others in the process. At 34%, health care workers are more engaged than their counterparts in the US workforce of whom only 29% are engaged. They motivate teams to press on and break through barriers when they face obstacles. Because they see the big picture they are very much aware of how their team members are doing. They focus on making sure that their team members have what they need to be successful. In so doing, they build strong loyalty within their team.

Summary Part I: Engagement and Target Fixation in Action

Motivating Altruistic Health Care Workers in a Data/Dollar Driven System

I worked with a health care organization recently that faced a dilemma. There was a significant disparity between the upper-level management and the front-line workers. The two groups were motivated by different core values. The upper-level managers were very focused on "data and dollars" while the front-line workers were very focused on the altruistic passion of making a difference. In health care, one cannot exist without the other. Wanting to make a difference is the real core of providing health care, but we rely on information and financially sustainable practices to deliver it consistently. Both parts are necessary. However, one of the quickest ways to disengage people that are motivated by altruism is to make it all about the money.

The Prescription to Engage Frontline Health Care Workers

Dan Pink, in his famous book *Drive*, shows us that people are motivated by three things: autonomy, mastery and purpose. Once people have their basic financial needs met, money is no longer a helpful motivator. Yet, we continue to try to motivate people by financial bonuses. Pink's work goes on to show us that in some cases, financial bonuses can actually result in decreased performance. Focusing on the financial aspects of care can have a notoriously bad impact on "purpose" driven frontline health care folks. They may assume that people that focus on dollars just do not get it. They may take it even one step further and believe that the leadership is trying to sabotage their ability to care for patients.

It is much more effective to motivate people in the trenches of health care by focusing on their passion to deliver better care, to be on the cutting edge of innovative care or to reach under-served populations more effectively. I recently had the opportunity to work with Elaine Couture, the Regional Chief Executive at Providence Health and Services. She and her upper management team have built a "mission driven" organization. The mission that permeates the organization to the very core is to take care of the poor and vulnerable. Yes, they still have to study "data and dollars", but they do so through the lens of their intense commitment to the mission. In doing so, they have significantly closed the gap between the upper management and the health care workers on the frontlines. Everyone knows that they need to focus on "data and dollars" so they can carry out the mission of taking care of the poor and vulnerable. Everyone gets it and that mission brings everyone together. Their employee and physician engagement numbers are impressive. Being mission driven makes a palpable difference.

Part II: Performance

*"Management is efficiency in
climbing the ladder of success;
leadership determines whether the
ladder is leaning against the right
wall."*

Stephen Covey

The Vertical View

Thus far in this book we have been discussing the horizontal plane of engagement which is helpful because it identifies the direction that people are facing and therefore the direction that they are moving. It identifies people that are moving in the wrong direction so that can be addressed. Once you identify people that are moving in the *right* direction, it is helpful to look at the vertical view of levels of performance. The passively disconnected and actively disengaged people do not even show up on this model. This is a model that specifically looks at how to *improve* engagement and impact.

Tier 4: Loyal Employees

"Get 'er done!"

Larry the Cable Guy

Performance Tiers

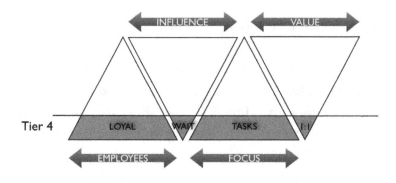

When we first arrived at the New Orleans Convention Center following Hurricane Katrina to set up the Medical Triage Unit, we didn't have enough staff. Our disaster team had originally been deployed to Lafayette to work in a shelter, but just a few hours after our arrival I had received a phone call from the Vice President of Medical Teams International. He was in the heart of New Orleans and asked me if I would be willing to split our team so that we could send half the team to the Convention Center. Agreeing to this, we arrived at 1:30 in the morning ready to do our best with only four people. I quickly recruited volunteers that were eager to help. One of the tasks that I assigned early on was that of being the "pharmacist". I needed someone that would organize all of our medications so that we could rapidly access them. I'm fairly certain that all of the local pharmacists either evacuated or were blown away by the storm. As we were setting up a woman named Sally said she was eager to help. She didn't have any medical background, but she was there and she was committed. I assigned her the task of organizing our medications alphabetically on a dingy old bookshelf that we found tossed out in the street and covered with muck. We brought the bookshelf in and she went to work. It wasn't long before she had the bookshelf all cleaned off and the medications organized alphabetically. She was then ready for her next task. We showed her how to count out the medications into small envelopes and gave her a pile of other supplies to organize. She wasn't focused on the big picture. She wasn't concerned about where the patients would go next or how they would get there. She was focused on organizing medications and dispensing them. Her job was invaluable. She was a great addition to the team. However, if something came up and she had to leave, it wouldn't have taken very long for her to in-service the next person to take her place.

Tier 4 represents the largest number of employees in any organization. Tier 4 Employees are like front-line soldiers in a battlefield. They rally to do whatever is asked of them and they take care of getting the details done. They wait to be told what to do and they do whatever is before them. They are loyal and dependable. It is impossible to get the job done without them. If someone says, "Hey, can you give me a hand over here?" they are the first to jump up to help. These are the ones that, in a horizontal view, are passively connected. They can have a very wide focus because they are task centric. Assign them any task and, as long as there is a manual that goes with it to explain the steps, they will get it done. However, their influence is limited because they wait to be told what to do. For the sake of comparison, I will assign them a value of one employee.

Tier 3: Engaged Employees

*"Any company trying to
compete...must figure out a way to
engage the mind of every employee."*

Jack Welch

Performance Tiers

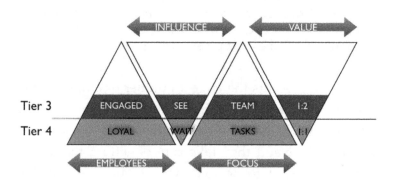

If you've ever watched the old television show MASH, you're already familiar with the radioman "Radar" O'Reilly. He was well known for being able to get anything for the doctors and nurses that served in the fictitious MASH unit located in Korea. Hawkeye Pierce, played by Alan Alda, and the rest of the gang came up with some of the most outlandish requests and Radar O'Reilly never let them down. So it was with Sgt. Sampson. I met him the first day that we arrived at the New Orleans Convention Center. He was loaned to us by the Nevada National Guard and given instructions to take care of us and get us whatever we needed. Talk about engaged! He was absolutely amazing. He carried one of those little reporter's spiral-bound notebooks in his front left pocket. He would come to me several times a day and say, "So Doc, what do you need? What can I get for you?". He would make some hasty scratches in his notebook and then disappear. He would hop on a helicopter and fly to the airport and begin to scrounge supplies for us. A short while later, he would return with whatever we'd asked for. It was absolutely stunning. He was fully engaged. He had the ability to see what we needed and he was focused on meeting the needs of our team. He never once complained. He never took his eyes off the goal of making sure that our team had everything that we needed to be able to deliver great medical care in a very stressful environment. He was exceedingly valuable to our team. In fact, he was worth at least two Tier 4 staff members. We would've had a difficult time accomplishing our goals without him. Our team was truly blessed by him. I can honestly say that he helped us save lives.

Not only are Tier 3 employees loyal but they are also engaged. There are fewer of them than Tier 4 employees. They have more influence than Tier 4 employees because they do not wait to be assigned a task. Their heads are up and they are looking to see how they can help. They are like the MVP on a basketball team. As well as taking care of the tasks at hand they are focused on the overall health of the team. They are worth at least two Tier 4 employees.

Tier 2: Empowered Employees

"Highly engaged employees make the customer experience. Disengaged employees break it."

Timothy R. Clark

Performance Tiers

I first met Bill Essig more than 30 years ago in the rural part of Northeast Thailand, when he was working for World Concern. My wife Debbie and I had been deployed with World Concern to work in a refugee camp serving the Hmong people that had been forced out of Laos and Vietnam. We didn't meet up with Bill again until years later when he was the Vice President of Medical Teams International. When Katrina decimated New Orleans, Bill was on one of the first planes into the heart of the disaster. He was searching to identify the area where our medical team could make the greatest impact. It was no easy feat to get into New Orleans in the first place. It involved crossing multiple police barricades and driving on roads made unsafe by trees and other scattered debris.

Bill has an uncanny gift of being able to identify opportunities for us to make a significant impact. He is focused on outcomes and unwilling to stop until he figures out the best strategy to accomplish our goals. Although he approaches his work with tremendous humility, he also approaches it with the confidence that he has the power to make a difference. He eventually connected with the Nevada National Guard at the Convention Center and offered to help. The Convention Center had just been chosen to be the only evacuation point for the entire city of New Orleans. Whether it is Katrina, hurricane Mitch in Honduras, the earthquake in Haiti or the devastating typhoon in the Philippines, Bill Essig has made a phenomenal impact through his insights, initiative, confidence and focus on outcomes.

Tier 2 people believe that they have the power to make a difference. They seek out opportunities and initiate solutions while tracking outcomes and, as a result, they have much more influence than Tier 3 or Tier 4 employees. Their relentless focus on outcomes makes them very productive. Overall, they are more valuable than five Tier 4 employees. Tier 2 employees are like a man with a treasure map. They can see where to go and start digging when they get there. They are focused on the outcome and do not stop until they find it.

Tier 1: Purposed Employees

> *"Here men from the planet earth first
> set foot upon the moon July 1969,
> A.D. We came in peace for all
> mankind"*
>
> *The plaque left on the Moon by Buzz
> Aldrin and Neil Armstrong*

Performance Tiers

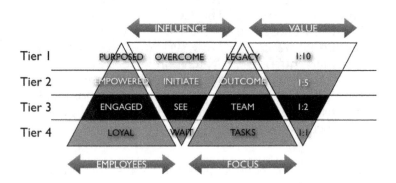

42

The first day that we arrived at the New Orleans Convention Center was jam-packed. We had people arriving by car, bus and pickup truck. We were operating out of tattered and torn tents that someone dropped off for us to use. The 82nd airborne had put up a secure perimeter. Patients were being searched on the way into the area. There were lines of people carrying what belongings they could. People were injured, people were dejected and sick people were without their medications.

On that first day, we added some doctors and nurses from Nashville and a few local emergency medical services (EMS) personnel that showed up to help. We set the area up like a typical triage unit. We had a triage funnel to categorize the patients and we used the traditional designations of green (for the walking wounded), yellow (for the moderately sick patients) and red (for the patients that were in critical condition).

One of the local EMS personnel had a blue shirt on that said New Orleans EMS on the front and PARAMEDIC in big bold letters on the back. I knew exactly where I wanted to assign her: to the red zone with the sickest patients. We needed another person that was capable of starting IVs on people that were sick. I was grateful to have someone with field experience. After working with her for about six hours, it became apparent that she was the smartest paramedic I'd ever worked with. She was amazing. I pulled one of the other New Orleans EMS personnel aside and asked him if Jullette really was a paramedic. He looked at me with a shocked expression on his face. Eyebrows raised, he said, "No man! She isn't a PARAMEDIC! That's Dr. Jullette Saussy! She's the Director of Emergency Medical Services for the entire city of New Orleans." Talk about feeling embarrassed, I wanted to crawl in a hole! After all, I trained in Seattle where the Director of Emergency Medical Services ran the program with an iron fist because he invented the Medic One program. Tripping over myself I went over to her right away and said, "Please forgive me! I had no idea that you are the Director of EMS for New Orleans. I work for you. My team works for you. This is your place. If you like, we will stand down. Use my staff and our equipment however you like. We belong to you." I will never forget her reply. It almost knocked me over. She looked me square in the eye and said, "You have no clue. We have begged God that he would send you! Don't you dare stand down! We have been working 18 to 20 hour days. Our communications have been cut off. We have been even been shot at by the very people we are trying to rescue. This has been unbelievable."

I told her that we were happy to help in any way that we could. She asked me to continue running the medical triage unit and said that she would come by as much as she could to help out. She explained that she had meetings around the city that she needed to attend as they tried to get their city back upon its feet. She was happy to have a place where she could come and practice medicine when she wasn't meeting with people to try to resuscitate their Emergency Medicine Services.

One thing still bothered me though. She was wearing a shirt that said PARAMEDIC. I couldn't help but ask her, "So what's with the shirt? What are you trying to do, throw off the out-of-town boys?" Even as I write this, her answer stops me in my tracks. "It's the only shirt that I have. You see I just bought a new home and hadn't had the time to move into it yet. Both of my homes were destroyed. This is all that I have left."

I just stood and stared. I was standing in the presence of a hero. A massive storm depleted her resources. At that point she believed that both of her homes had been destroyed (she later found out that they were salvageable). There she was, living on the street. Communications had been destroyed by the storm. She had to rally her courageous team of paramedics and EMTs to improvise and provide services. Paramedics were no longer able to talk to the physicians at the hospital. They were on their own. There was no dispatch. They had to go out to the communities that they served to take care of the needs as they found them. Dr. Saussy was purpose driven. She overcame tremendous obstacles in the midst of our nation's greatest natural disaster to deliver services to people that desperately needed their help. Dr. Saussy had a laser-like focus and, as a result, left an undeniable legacy. It is hard to place a value on someone like that. She saved the lives of hundreds of people if not more.

Tier 1 employees are, unfortunately, rare. Their purpose driven motivation is nearly impossible to stop.

Simon Sinek's TED Talk, "How Great Leaders Inspire Action", is consistently listed in the top 10 TED talks of all time. In his talk he illustrates how the most effective organizations have at their very core the concept of *Why?* The most effective organizations are able to overcome obstacles because they know why they are doing what they are doing. The focus is much more on the *Why* than it is on the *What* they do. The same is true for individuals. The most effective people in the workplace are the people that are driven by the *Why* that is deep within. Tier 1 employees are like the NASA team and astronauts involved in the Apollo 13 challenge. When the tank on the Apollo 13 ruptured and put the lives of the crew members and the entire mission in jeopardy, they rallied and overcame tremendous odds to bring the astronauts home. They had an unstoppable *Why*. If you know your *Why*, you will figure out the *How*. Because Tier 1 people are purpose driven, they overcome the obstacles that they encounter. They get things done. They leave a legacy. Value to the organization? 10 times more than a Tier 4 employee.

Summary Part II: Engagement is Not Enough

The instructions on a fire extinguisher seem to be a bit simplistic and obvious, until you have to actually use one to put out a fire. In reality, the instructions are actually counterintuitive. When the fire happens, most people are overwhelmed with the flames. It seems natural to grab a fire extinguisher and point it at the flames hoping that the fire will go out. The instructions on the fire extinguisher tell us, however, to point the fire extinguisher at the base of the flames. That is where the fire originates. It is not necessarily obvious because it may not be glowing. There's been a lot written over the past several years about the importance of employee engagement. In order to move people to higher tiers of engagement it is necessary to take a deeper look to discover *why* people are not engaged in the first place. We need to look at the base of the flames and take a look at mindset.

Part III: Mindset

Mindset: Power and Purpose

Screaming at George Bush!

It's been over 10 years since Katrina but some images haven't faded a bit. One of them is an interview that I saw on CNN. A large woman was standing with her feet planted and unwilling to move. She was holding her little daughter's hand as she was being interviewed. Actually, it wasn't much of an interview. She was screaming so loud that the reporter almost ducked. "When is George Bush going to bring me my food!"

I quietly whispered back, "He's not".

It took me a while to figure out why her interview was so disturbing to me. Obviously she believed that George Bush had all the power and she had none. What bothered me more than that was that she was not asking, "When is George Bush going to bring my *daughter* some food?"

Not everyone took her approach. Plenty did, that is for sure. But some did not. Some, despite losing everything they owned, were actually pitching in and helping. It is amazing how disasters strip away all of the fluff. People's motives are exposed and much easier to spot when they do not have anything to hide behind. So what causes some people to cave in and give up while others dig in and leave a legacy? It became clear as day that mindset has something to do with outcomes.

Two Dimensions

It is important at this point to make the clarification that we are talking about types of mindsets and not different types of people. Tagging people with labels such as "victim" can be counterproductive. They can be helpful, however, to identify mindsets. The distinction is important because we all vacillate back and forth between different types of mindsets. We are not "one or the other". We have a choice on what mindset we use.

In order to understand how victims think it is necessary to consider two different dimensions: power and purpose. In 1953 Julian Rotter developed the concept of locus of control. He defined victims as having an external locus of control. They believe that all power exists external to them, and things happened *to* them. If they had a bumper sticker it would say "Stuff Happens!" And in small print underneath it would say, "To me!". And then, in fine print under that it would say, "All the time!". We have all had the opportunity to work with people that use this mindset. They consume energy. In fact, they demand energy. Energy flows towards them.

The second dimension has to do with purpose. Disasters strip away the fluff and people are exposed. Their strategies are clearly revealed. It is easy to see that at the rawest level a victim's purpose is to take. They approach the world believing in scarcity. They believe that the world works on a disaster economy that says resources are scarce and there is not enough to go around. As a result, they feel almost a panic and a desperate drive to gather resources and store them. After all, they think, things could get worse. Their underlying motto is "Help *me!*" with a big emphasis on "me". Consequently, they not only consume energy because of their external locus of control, but they consume resources as well. Their underlying emotion and motivation is fear.

The Victim Mindset makes you a Powerless Taker.

The Thriver Matrix

The Victim Mindset

> *"When is George Bush going to bring
> me **my** food?"*
>
> *Katrina Victim*

A Steak Sandwich Worth Dying For

The Victim Mindset dramatically impacted the
relief effort in New Orleans after Katrina. The
disaster was just too massive and the relief teams
couldn't get to everyone fast enough. The woman
and her daughter were just one example. There
were people stranded on bridges and overpasses
just waiting and waiting for someone else to do

something. Truck (a nickname he earned for obvious reasons) decided that he wasn't going to evacuate because he had "been through these hurricanes before". He told me that he was just going to stay home and "have myself a steak sandwich". When the levee broke he was sitting at the bar in his house with his sandwich and fries. He told me that he heard a loud "boom!" and then looked down find that the water was at his feet. Before he got off his stool, the water was at his ankles. He grabbed his sandwich and fries and headed up the stairs. His eyes got big as he told me, "The water kept coming up; it kept coming up." Terrified, he eventually ended up climbing the stairs up into in his attic. But the water followed him up the stairs. "The water kept coming up; it kept coming up." With no way out of the attic, he started kicking at the boards in the roof but couldn't get them to budge. He began to panic. Feeling around in the water he finally found a sledge hammer and knocked a hole in the roof. He crawled out through the hole and just sat there powerless. He ate his steak sandwich, nibbled on his fries, and "waited for the man with the boat".

Why You Should Care

We encounter the Victim's Mindset in health care in two different scenarios. When health care workers talk about victims, the first thing that usually comes to mind are patients. There are plenty of stories about patients that are unwilling to accept responsibility for their own health care. The financial impact of the Victim Mindset in patients on the global cost of medicine is almost beyond comprehension. Certainly, many of the concepts addressed in this book apply directly to patients as well, but that would require another book altogether.

The other form of the Victim's Mindset encountered in health care can be found within health care workers themselves. Some people perceive themselves as being powerless in the midst of these rapidly changing times. They can start to feel alone, isolated and at risk. It is not long before people with the Victim's Mindset will begin to stockpile resources.

They become like a man in a lifeboat with a hole in it:

1. The hole demands his attention
2. His boat requires constant bailing
3. His boat moves more slowly
4. His fear becomes contagious

The irony is, if he rescued someone else he would have someone to plug the hole, be able to get the water out more effectively, move more quickly and save more people. Then it would be hope that was contagious.

The Bystander Mindset

*"The world is a dangerous place to
live, not because of those who do evil,
but because of those who look on and
do nothing."*

Albert Einstein

No Stories, Only Regrets

At this point in the book I would like to share with you some of the stories from bystanders.

BLANK

However, bystanders don't have any stories; they only have regrets.

When I have conversations with people about the work that I do during disasters they often reply, "I sure wish that I could do something to help." Their heart is in the right place but they do not believe that they have the power to make a difference. Unfortunately, what they do not understand is that they actually *can* make a difference. Bystanders mistakenly assume that the only people that can help are the "professionals". It is a myth that only trained professionals can make a difference. Research shows that in the earliest phase after a disaster the first people to help are the people on the scene. Who knows if they will be professionals or not – it is just

55

whoever happens to be there. People using the Bystander Mindset, on the other hand, stand by paralyzed with the belief that they just do not have what it takes.

The Bystander Mindset makes you a Powerless Giver.

Why You Should Care

As we have already discussed, a total of 53% of the health care workforce is either Passively Disconnected or, at best, Passively Connected. These are the bystanders that show up to work, clock in, put their time in, clock out and go home. The cycle repeats but they do not contribute much more than the basics. Imagine the impact of converting only half of these bystanders to become fully engaged employees! The impact on HCAHPS (Consumer Assessment of Health Care Providers and Systems) scores could be profound. I experienced what this could look like recently when my wife was hospitalized. One of my greatest memories of the entire experience was when one of the housekeepers came in, introduced herself and asked if there was anything that she could do to help. She cleaned the room, again asked if there was anything else that she could do to help, and then went to get my wife some extra blankets. She certainly did not come in to work as a bystander.

Like spectators watching a game from home, Bystanders care about the outcome but they do not have any influence over it. Bystanders can also be like a non-dominant hand; they underestimate their potential contribution until that hand is extended to rescue someone else.

The Manipulator Mindset

"Forget about her! She's just trash!
Come and get us!"

Katrina Survivor

Cathy's Story

Cathy was a single mother of two under the age of three. As Hurricane Katrina was headed straight for New Orleans, the mayor announced an evacuation. For Cathy this was an impossibility. She lived paycheck to paycheck and barely had enough money for both diapers and food. She did not own a car. She did not have any money that she could use for transportation to evacuate. It just wasn't possible. With her deep commitment to never abandon her children she decided that she would hunker down in her second-story apartment and ride out the storm. As the wind began to blow harder and harder she decided she was going to need to move from the living room into the bathroom with her children. The windows in her living room broke out a short while after that. The noise was horrendous. Her children screamed all night long. It was a terrifying experience. The next morning there was an eerie calm. Opening the bathroom door she found her living room to be a disaster. There was glass everywhere and everything was wet. All the magazines that were on the tables and all the

57

decorations had been blown around the apartment. Feeling overwhelmed she had an intense desire to just get out of the apartment. She grabbed her two daughters and the stroller and headed out.

There was debris everywhere. People were walking around outside with dazed looks on their faces. Cathy was just happy that she and her daughters had survived. She had pushed the stroller for a couple of blocks when she heard a terrible noise. She looked up just in time to see a gigantic wall of water heading straight for her and her daughters. She spun the stroller around and began to sprint back to her apartment. Before she knew it, the water had caught up to her. In an instant the water was up to her knees. She kept trying to push through the water but it was just too deep, and getting deeper. She grabbed her two daughters out of the stroller as the water carried it away. She began to run as fast as she could through the water to get back to her second-story apartment. She figured if they could just get there they should be safe. Still the water continued to rise. As she got to the intersection, one block away from her apartment, she spotted one of the traffic control boxes that control the streetlights. Fighting to save her daughters, she fought her way over to it and put her two daughters up on top of the control box. Still the water continued to rise. It didn't take long for her to realize that she was going to drown if she did not get on top of the control box as well. Sitting with one daughter on either side of her on top of the control box she thought that she was safe. Still the water continue to rise. She had to pick her daughters up and put put them on her shoulders. The water finally stopped rising when it got to the middle of her chest.

"I will never abandon my children!"

She sat there waiting to be rescued... for four days!

There was no rest. If she fell asleep for only a moment, her daughters would die. The agony and fear were incomprehensible.

On the afternoon of the fourth day, a 17-foot aluminum boat with 17 people in it appeared. As they paddled their way over to her, she whispered "Just take my babies." Although the boat was tremendously overloaded, the people in the boat said, "No, we will take you and your babies, but please be careful getting into the boat."

As she began to pass her daughters to the people in the boat, the most peculiar and horrific event began to unfold. Across the street from the people in the boat there were four people on top of the roof of one of the buildings. They begin to yell down to the people in the boat, "Forget that woman! She's just trash! Come and get us!" Shocked, the people and the boat yelled back, "Women and children first! We'll come back and get you next trip." The people on the roof yelled back, "We've got food! We've got money! We've got water! Come and get us! She's just trash!" Once again, the people in the boat yelled back, "Women and children first! We'll come and get you next trip." Then the unthinkable happened. BAM! BAM! BAM! The people on the roof began to shoot at the people in the boat!

Fortunately, the people on the roof did not know how to shoot very well. Nobody was injured. Cathy was able to pass her children to the people in the boat and then carefully get in the boat herself. They rapidly paddled around the corner

and out of sight. After four days of terror, Cathy
and her daughters were finally safe once again.

While I suspect that you have never had anyone
shoot at you with a gun, most people have been shot at
in one way or another. We have been on the receiving
end of an email that was shot at us. We have been on the
receiving end of a look that was shot at us. And, we
have been on the receiving end of a comment that was
shot at us. Not only does it not feel good but it definitely
has an adverse impact on the relationship dynamics. It
seems like common sense to avoid shooting at the very
people that are essential for survival, but people using
the Manipulator Mindset lack that insight. It is as if no
one ever told them the foundational truth, "If you need
to be rescued by the people in a boat, don't shoot at
them."

People that choose to use the Manipulator Mindset
believe that they have the power to make a difference
and that it is all about them. When people use the
Manipulator Mindset they often times do not realize
how they impact other people. They do not start out
with the idea of offending others. They simply believe
that they have no other option.

Disaster Economy Thinking

Similar to the Victim Mindset, the Manipulator
Mindset has at its very core the concept of disaster
economy. It is a fear based economy that focuses on the
needs of self. When resources become scarce, the

Manipulator mindset demands its share of the resources and even more. They believe that they will get more if they take more. It is a one-way street and it all flows toward them. They are not content with what they have and so they begin hoarding resources. You can often hear them mumbling to themselves, "If I don't look out for #1, who else will?"

After Katrina, the news showed us over and over that those with the Manipulator Mindset were stealing big screen TVs from Walmart. It looked like they were getting ahead for a while. It did not occur to me until years later that they had no place to plug them in. Other people will only tolerate the self-centered strategies of the Manipulator Mindset for so long. The truth is:

"If you look out for #1, no one else will."

Dan Diamond, MD

A manipulator is like a drowning man that pushes his rescuer under in order to get his own head above water. Manipulators abuse and destroy the very people that can save them. They are sometimes so focused on their own needs that they do not realize that they are even using the Manipulator Mindset. The Manipulator Mindset is just a mindset. It is a strategy that people use. It is important to remember that it is not a type of person. Sometimes this mindset can be a bit subtle, in fact. The Manipulator Mindset is not just used by people with bullets and guns. In the workplace it shows

61

up in body language, behaviors, words and control, but the impact can be just as negative.

The Manipulator Mindset makes you a Powerful Taker.

Why You Should Care

The federal government means business when it comes to decreasing unacceptably high rates of hospital acquired conditions (HACs). They recently cut Medicare payments to 721 hospitals—totaling $371 million—and fined 2,610 hospitals for having too many readmissions. The hospitals that have been most successful in decreasing these penalties have been the ones that change the way that they deliver care. Unfortunately, people with the Manipulator Mindset tend to hate change. They try to protect their turf and undermine the work of others that they see as a threat. They take any suggestion of improvement as a criticism of the way they are doing things. Moving these people to fight for you and not against you has a profound impact on the overall success of the organization.

The Thriver Mindset

*"My mission in life is not merely to
survive, but to thrive; and to do so
with some passion, some compassion,
some humor, and some style."*

Maya Angelou

Sergeant Bailey's Story

The air was humid and thick but the wind was
still. Sergeant Bailey was up early in the morning
glad that Hurricane Katrina had spared New
Orleans. The weather service had been predicting
for days that the hurricane was going to hit the
city of New Orleans head on. As the world held its
breath, at the very last moment the hurricane
veered eastward and came ashore in Mississippi.
The newspapers proclaimed that New Orleans
had been spared once again and Sgt. Bailey knew
that it was time to begin the hard work of getting
out and cleaning up his yard. Large oak branches
had fallen and were all around his yard.

As he was hauling one of the large branches he
was startled by loud noise that came from down
the street. As he turned to look, he was not
prepared for what he saw. He told me that it
looked like a large "wall of water" that was
rushing towards him. He described it as
something out of a B rated movie. I think at this
point my first reaction would have been to run as
fast as I could. As a police officer, Sgt. Bailey's
biggest concern was to get to the trunk of his car
so he could remove his weapons and place them
in a secret hiding place located in his attic. As he
put his key into the trunk, he was nearly knocked

63

down by the water. He grabbed his weapons and headed into the house. He ran up two flights of stairs to his attic. As he tucked his weapons into the secret hiding place and turned around, he discovered that the water had quietly followed him up the two flights of stairs.

It was a defining moment as he stood and debated whether or not to continue up into his attic, or swim two stories down and hope that he could make it out the door before he drowned. After a brief debate he decided to swim because the water was continuing to rise and the attic was looking more and more like a deadly option. He took a couple of deep breaths and dove down. He swam down the first flight of stairs, turned at the landing and then continued on down the second flight of stairs. He swam across the entryway and went through the front door. He shot up next to the house and came up gasping for air as he grasped the gutters that just moments ago were two stories above the ground. He caught his breath and then swung his leg up and climbed onto the roof.

His police radio was still on his belt and miraculously the radio still worked. He keyed the microphone and notified the central communications (CENCOM) operator that he was stranded on his roof and that the levee had just broken. He requested assistance as soon as possible. The operator replied that they would send someone to help him as soon as they could, but they were completely overwhelmed. He described what happened next to me as the most painful experience of his entire life. He listened as his colleagues called the operator and begged for help. They said that they were stranded with their families and couldn't get out of their homes and that the water was rising. Just about then, his radio crackled and went completely dead. He was cut off from the outside world. What he didn't realize at the time was that communications for the entire city of New Orleans —fire, police, emergency medical services—had been completely cut off. No one had anticipated flooding of this magnitude. The radio equipment for CENCOM was located on the 1st floor. This was a costly mistake. Under siege from the biggest natural disaster our nation had ever faced, the emergency responders from the city of New Orleans were completely cut off from their communications network.

Sgt. Bailey estimates that he stayed on his roof for somewhere between 10 and 12 hours. Pacing back and forth on the roof he debated whether or not to wait for rescue or try to swim for safety. He did not know at that point how large the flood was or how long he would have to swim. The water was full of debris and contamination. In contrast to the water found in a lake or swimming pool, this water looked more like that found in an outhouse. It was dank and nasty. He finally came to terms with the fact that if he was going to become part of the solution he was going to have to jump in with both feet. (Sound like your job?)

He swam to his neighbor's home and grabbed onto the gutters to catch his breath. He then swam to another neighbor's home and climbed up on top of his van. Leaning forward with his hands on his knees he paused to catch his breath. As he continued to swim he became more determined to press on and find a way out. Overall, he estimates that he swam at least a mile before finally coming upon a Vietnamese gentleman and his wife in their 17-foot aluminum boat. As they grabbed him and pulled him into the boat, a new friendship

65

had begun. The three of them spent the next three days rescuing people. They saved the lives of hundreds and hundreds of people, including Cathy with her two babies that had been stranded on a traffic control box for four days.

I wonder how the story would've been different if the Vietnamese couple had said to themselves, "We are just immigrants and don't speak the language very well. What could we offer?" What if they had just stayed home?

It is amazing what can be done by people who believe they have the power to make a difference and are willing to put their own lives at risk to invest in the lives of others. When this happens in the business world, it goes against the conventional wisdom that says that everyone has to look out for themselves. In fact, employees that believe that they have the power to make a difference, that choose to put the needs of others in front of their own, become the most valuable employees in an organization. They are the ones that everyone fights to keep because they are committed to making their team members successful. They become the most valued, sought after and most effective members of the team.

Abundance Economy Thinking

"Perhaps it's no longer time for me to be served."

Brandon Cameron

People with the Thriver Mindset believed that they have the power to make a difference and that it is not all about them. They choose to go out and make this difference in service to others. In marked contradiction to the manipulators, they do not even consider what they will end up with. In fact, they actually will end up with more if they give away what they have, but that is certainly not their driving force. They believe in investing in the welfare of other people and they try to make other people look good.

The Thriver Mindset makes you a Powerful Giver.

The Thriver Matrix

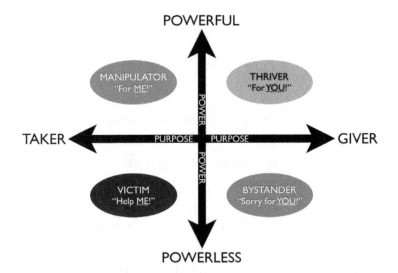

Why You Should Care

People that choose the Thriver Mindset rapidly move up the tiers of employee engagement because they are willing to give and put others first. Because they are not focused on themselves they see the value of serving their team. When they see a job that needs to be done they do not slump back and say, "Someone should do something to help those people!" They jump up and try to actually *do* something about it.

Growing a Culture of Heroes

"The way to get things done is not to mind who gets the credit."

Benjamin Jowett

One of the hallmarks of someone using the Thriver Mindset is that they do whatever they can to make other people successful. In other words, their strategy is to do whatever they can to make other people into heroes. They are more concerned with making an impact than they are with who gets the credit. Their efforts are contagious and may eventually transform an entire organization.

Transition to Thriving

Moving Bystanders to Thrivers

Bystanders are undoubtedly the easiest to move. The reason that they are the easiest to move is because their hearts are already in the right place. They already have a desire to make a difference. They already see the need and wish that someone could help. They just do not believe that they themselves have the power to make a difference. The easiest way to move someone with the Bystanders Mindset to the Thriver Mindset is through mentorship. Coming alongside of them and saying, "I know that you have a heart to help. Let me show you how," is all that it generally takes. It can be a very empowering experience for them to spend time with a mentor as they learn how to make a difference themselves. This does not need to be a formal complicated mentorship program. Managers can spot employees that are engaged and thriving and ask them if they would informally be willing to come alongside and mentor an employee with the Bystander Mindset. The impact of this is contagious. Soon, those that previously used the Bystander Mindset see the impact of what they are doing, feel better about their work and become excited to help other people on their team as well.

Moving Manipulators to Thrivers

Manipulators are motivated by fear and, at times, greed. Both of these emotions are a result of disaster economy thinking. They believe that there will not be enough to go around and so they need to grab what they can, while they can. They believe that they deserve resources more than others. They do not consider the impact on other people. Consequently, the impact of people with the Manipulators Mindset can be disastrous. It does not take very many to bring down the enthusiasm, initiative and commitment of an entire team. It is essential to either remove them from the organization or convert them from the Manipulator Mindset to the Thriver Mindset.

Because those with the Manipulator Mindset often operate from a position of fear and defensiveness, they will not respond well to the suggestion of counseling.

From their perspective they believe, "I don't have a problem, there's nothing wrong with me!" They require a unique approach. The most effective way to convert those with the Manipulator Mindset is through coaching. They will only receive input from someone that they trust and a professional coach can be viewed as someone that will help them improve their success. A coach can gradually nudge them into taking small risks of investing in the success of others. As trust is built, the issue of the scarcity disaster economy can be addressed. It is usually not true that there is a scarcity of resources, and once they realize this they can gradually be shifted to an abundance economy. As they experience the contagious joy of investing in others, they gradually shift away from taking to giving.

Moving Victims to Thrivers

People in the Victim Mindset can be the most difficult to change to the Thriver Mindset, as they have to move along both axes of the Thriver Matrix. Occasionally they can move themselves like my Medical Assistant, Dana, did. When she considered the Thriver's Matrix, she recognized her unhealthy mindset immediately. For the first time she saw that her strategy was that of the Victim. With renewed vision she then went on to make significant changes in both her locus of control as well as her purpose. Interestingly, her job satisfaction soared. She started working on helping others to be successful by believing that she could make a difference. She enjoyed her job as she discovered newfound purpose.

71

The rest of the team also found her to be a delight. In fact, she went on to become the most valuable member of the team. Everyone appreciated her because she was helping them to become successful.

Not everyone with the Victim Mindset will experience such a rapid transition, however. They have to change two different dimensions: power and purpose. In my experience, those who tend to use the Victim Mindset respond well to counseling. In order to make a significant shift, they need to explore both their locus of control as well as issues of trust. If they are unwilling or unable to do counseling, a supportive co-worker or manager could come alongside and get them involved in projects that focus on the needs of others. For example, "I would like you to work on a project with me where we explore some creative ways that, as nurses, we could make the radiology department become more successful in their throughput times." This will get the person with the Victim Mindset to start asking the "So, what keeps you up at night?" question of the radiology department. They could then start looking for opportunities to make a difference. Giving them responsibilities that they will have a high success rate at is also a good way to build their confidence in being able to help others. It is important to help them see the impact of their work and recognize their accomplishments.

The Individual Mindset and the Team Mindset

Mindset forms the foundation for and ultimately determines the impact that will be made for both individuals and teams. Every team that I have been a part of has had a different personality and yet the most effective teams all had the same mindset: The Thriver Mindset. With the right mindset they not only overcame obstacles that stopped others in their tracks, but they made the other teams around them more successful as well. People used to measure the success of teams by what they got: recognition, money, promotions. Success in the silo is no longer good enough. Now teams must be judged by what they give. The most effective teams focus on how they can make everyone within their sphere of influence successful. When they approach problems, they see them from a three dimensional viewpoint and therefore make an amplified impact on the world around them.

Summary Part III: Mindset Matters

"Everything can be taken from a man but one thing: the last of human freedoms – to choose one's attitude in any given set of circumstances, to choose one's own way."

Viktor E. Frankl

Mindset is the catalyst for significance...or not. Three of the four mindsets negatively impact others. Only the Thriver Mindset leads to a life of significance and legacy. Fortunately, we *always* have the ability to choose how we will respond. Viktor Frankl, the Austrian neurologist and psychiatrist that spent seven years in Nazi concentration camps, said, "Between stimulus and response there is a space. In that space is our power to choose our response. In our response lies our growth and our freedom." When considering mindset there are two essential questions that we must ponder on an ongoing, daily basis:

1. Will I choose to be powerless or powerful in this situation?
2. Will I choose to be a giver or a taker in this situation?

The answer to those two questions define our mindset and the impact that we will have. Believe that you can make a difference and choose to put others first and you will discover that you will have a lasting positive legacy on your sphere of influence

Part IV: Problem Solving

"Good planning is important. I've also regarded a sense of humor as one of the most important things on a big expedition. When you're in a difficult or dangerous situation, or when you're depressed about the chances of success, someone who can make you laugh eases the tension."

Edmund Hillary, first climber to summit Mount Everest

Three Tools for Better Thinking

Maximize Your Brain's Ability to Solve Problems Under Pressure

Dave Gray, Sunni Brown, and James Macanufo — in their book *Gamestorming: A Playbook for Innovators, Rulebreakers, and Changemakers* — describe three types of thinking: divergent, emergent and convergent. They use the analogy of a pencil sharpened at both ends. It starts with a point, levels out for a while and ends with a different point.

The Model

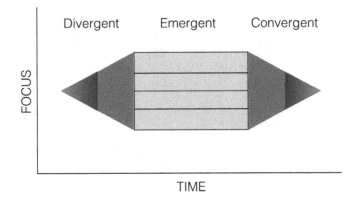

Adapted from Dave Gray and Sunni Brown and James Macanufo, *Gamestorming: A Playbook for Innovators, Rulebreakers, and Changemakers* [Kindle Edition]. loc. 894

Starting from the first point, the pencil expands and widens. Early in the creative process it is helpful to use divergent thinking. Divergent thinking has a broad field of view. It is like looking through a wide angle lens on a camera. It is a high energy type of thinking. As your brain sees the world through this expansive view, it begins to look for patterns and connections. In the process, new ideas start to emerge and we discover possibilities that we hadn't considered before. Humor is very important during this phase. It seems counterintuitive or perhaps it may appear to be even morally wrong to bring humor into a difficult situation like a disaster. However, it can be the key to discovering the best solutions. In fact, when I recruit members for our disaster team, one of the most important skills that I look for is a sense of humor. Frequently we get deployed into situations that are not what we think they are going to be. We need to remain nimble and agile on our feet. In order to do that, humor is essential. Besides, it is more fun.

Sometimes the question, "What's so funny?" can actually be the first step to discovering a solution. There were plenty of funny things to laugh at after Hurricane Katrina. I suspect that for some of these you had to be there to understand the humor, please try to use your imagination. I saw a woman swallow a live snake, pull it back out and swallow it again. No kidding. I also thought that I knew what a full portable outhouse looked like before Katrina. I now have a completely different picture in my mind. There was also the man that showed up with an entire duffel bag full of swords thinking that he was going to be able to evacuate with his weapons... on a military helicopter! Sometimes, you just have to chuckle.

Laughter is good for your brain. It energizes your thinking and allows your brain to see new ideas. It is the fuel for creativity. We were constantly forced to improvise as we provided care at the New Orleans Convention Center and finding some humor in the midst of it all allowed us to keep our head in the game and make a difference. Using humor in difficult situations is like tilling hard soil. You are much more likely to get something to grow if you break up the ground a bit. You still need seeds and water, but it is hard to get much done without first tilling the soil.

Emergent thinking is the next phase. This is the phase where ideas are considered and kicked around. The goal of this phase is to consider feasibility, costs, strengths, weaknesses, opportunities and threats (SWOT Analysis). It is a levelheaded approach to the mound of ideas gathered during the divergent phase. This is an important part of the problem solving process and without it, the team becomes vulnerable to unforeseen complications. It is a time to be sure that the less vocal members of the team voice their opinions and insights. (Often times, they need to be specifically asked.) During this time of considering options, new hybrid insights often emerge as we mix and match components and ideas.

Convergent thinking is focused. In the pencil model, it is bringing everything together to a sharp point. In fact, convergent thinking can be most helpful when it is narrowed and down to business. In contrast to divergent thinking which is linked to humor, convergent thinking is tied to a more somber mood. If it occurs too early in the process, convergent thinking can block ideas, yet it is essential to use it later in the process. Without it, nothing would ever get done. Convergent thinking demands focus and precipitates action.

It is important to use these types of thinking strategically and in order. Start with divergent thinking to discover possible solutions. Move to emergent thinking to refine and sort them out. Then, finally, use convergent thinking to weed out the chaff and focus on the measurable specifics of implementation.

The problem is, since these thinking styles are linked to mood, when people are depressed or under pressure they tend to default to the style of thinking that matches their mood – convergent thinking. Using convergent thinking at the outset can block vision and obscure viable solutions. It can shut down creativity and limit options. However, there is a place for convergent thinking. It can and should be used very effectively to drive focus at the end of the problem solving process. Again, recall the model of the pencil. Start with the problem and use divergent thinking to discover possible solutions. Then use emergent thinking to process the various ideas and choose the best option. Once that is done, use the laser focus of convergent thinking to get the job done. Having awareness of which style of thinking you are in at any given time allows you to intentionally choose them to break through barriers and get things done.

Get it Wrong: Waste Time and Miss Opportunities.

Here is the problem: When most of us encounter challenges or difficulties, we tend to become discouraged. As we have noted, discouragement promotes convergent thinking. This happens frequently during disasters. People become so focused on the problem that they miss opportunities to find a solution. The more discouraged they get, the more convergent their thinking becomes. It can become a vicious cycle. Limited vision leads to deeper problems which leads to more discouragement which leads to more limited vision. Using humor can be very helpful but it needs to be done strategically. Use it on purpose early in the process but tone it down during the implementation phase because it can be disruptive when people are trying to focus and get things done.

Get it Right: Improve Versatility. Discover Solutions. Focus Resources.

The pencil model is a helpful one. Remember the three phases and be sure to keep things moving. Staying in divergent mode is not helpful. There is a time to set aside the humor to get the work done. There is a time for convergent, focused thinking. What the model does not show, however, is that this is a cyclical process. Throughout the day, when we are in a disaster setting, we repeat the process of divergent thinking, emergent thinking and convergent thinking. Learn to recognize the three types of thinking within yourself and with your team. Next time you're stuck, try using humor. Look around to see what is so funny. Challenge your team to laugh. Kick around some of the ideas that you have during the emergent phase and bring the process to an actionable conclusion using convergent thinking.

Disaster-Improv

"Along the road to success, there are many tempting parking places."

Will Rogers

Street Performers and Disasters

I put myself through medical school as a street mime...one of the nice ones. I saw my first street mime at the Spokane World's Fair and I was intrigued. I have always enjoyed story telling but here was someone doing it without words. In the midst of my intense studies in medical school, mime helped me stay in touch with the outside world. It was good for my brain to be creative. It did not take long for me to integrate it into the practice of medicine. I am much more aware of nonverbal communication. I also benefited tremendously from the principles of improv. As a street performer, improv is essential. Without it, my audience would simply just walk away. Looking back after over 30 years of international disaster medicine, it has become clear that I did not learn all that I needed about problem solving in medical school. I learned some of it on the street. The concept of Disaster-Improv comes from the mashing together of these two very unique schools. Combining the discipline of medicine with the creative improv of street mime leads to very agile, innovative and responsive solutions that meet the need when times are tough and it matters most. Disaster-Improv can be broken down into three distinct phases: See, Sort and Solve.

See

The first phase of Disaster-Improv sounds simple enough on the surface. To the contrary, *See* is anything but simple. It involves perceiving with the right depth and asking the right questions. Most often, this phase uses divergent thinking. Moving ahead without taking the time to stop to understand, consider the risks and discover the available resources can lead to ineffective efforts or even put the team at risk. In the next chapter, we will take a deep dive to look at what *See* is all about.

Sort

Sorting out priorities is the second phase of the process. This is the phase where needs are defined and risks and resources are outlined. We need to decide which of our challenges are the most important to deal with immediately and which can be tackled later. Most often, this phase uses emergent thinking. Once the priorities are at least preliminarily outlined, it is time to move to the third phase.

Solve

We have established what our problems are, and which are the highest priority, now we need to come up with solutions and carry them out. Most often, this phase uses convergent thinking. The *Solve* phase includes putting together a plan and acting on it. It is not enough to just put together a plan and study it. It is essential that the plan is acted on. It also needs to be acted on with the understanding that *Solve* may not be the final phase. In fact, most of the time it is not the final phase because this is a cyclical model. It is hard to get it right the first time when in a high pressure environment. The process repeats itself until an acceptable solution is reached.

The Essential Rule Behind Disaster-Improv

At the very core of Disaster-Improv lies a key principle that is so essential that it could actually be considered the *Law* of Disaster-Improv. This may be worth writing down and posting it where you can see it every morning. The Law of Disaster-Improv is this:

"There is no such thing as failure, only feedback."

To believe otherwise is counterproductive and sometimes outright destructive. Often, after the first time around the loop, we find out the hard way that the plan fell short or, even worse, may have backfired altogether. In an unpredictable environment, things can easily get worse before they get better. It may in fact take *several* times around the loop to get to an acceptable solution. The key is to understand that the process is cyclical. After the *Solve* phase comes another *See* phase. Part of the *See* phase in the second (or third or fourth) time around is "seeing" what you have learned. It is a little like being in the school of hard knocks. In regular school you learn and then take the test. In the school of hard knocks, you take the test and *then* learn. In this school, there is no failing grade unless you do not try to do anything at all. Approach these difficult situations with the strategy of "I will try something and see what I learn." If you are fortunate and solve the problem after the first time around, great! Frequently, it takes more that one trip around.

Yes, and

It is worth mentioning here that one of the key tenants of improvisational theater is the idea of "Yes, and". On stage (or on the street) nothing ends creativity faster than someone saying "No". It is much more helpful to say "Yes, and...". At first it may seem a bit awkward, but it forces us to think differently and look for opportunities to contribute rather than cut-off. Using the Thriver Mindset of powerful giving it is much easier to discover ways to move the "scene" forward.

For example, how many times have you heard this conversation:

Staff Member: "We need more staff!"

Manager (having just been knocked around in a budget meeting): "No, our budget won't allow it."

End of discussion. With enthusiasm and creativity squashed, the staff member walks away thinking, "What the heck, I do not know why I even try. They never listen to me." If this happens too many times, the staff member will be at risk of disengaging and then just "showing up" at work to get a paycheck.

Using "Yes, and..." the conversation might head in a different direction. It might go something like this:

Staff member: "We need more staff!"

Manager: "Yes, and we need to be sure to get them at the right time to be able to meet the variable need. I have been kicking around some ideas. Tell me more about what you're thinking."

The conversation may eventually produce some new ideas about variable staffing that may actually meet the need without increasing the budget. The staff member comes away from the conversation feeling that she was listened to and that her idea was valued. She may in fact share a new creative solution with her manager because she has taken the time to ask her boss, "So what keeps you up at night?" She is very aware that the budget is tight so she has been kicking around some ideas that she understands have been very effective at a hospital in Australia.

The Model

DISASTER-IMPROV™

SEE   SORT

SOLVE

Get it Wrong: The Story Becomes Shorter and the Outcomes Less Desirable.

It is easy to fail. Some people fail before they even start. They consider the gap between where they are and where they want to be, and say that it is too big. Some folks try one attempt around the loop and walk away in defeat. Staying focused only on the problem and on themselves, they walk away and embarrassingly say, "I'll never do that again!" When their focus stayed on the problem, they do not even see any potential solutions. Remember, discouragement can lead to convergent thinking that limits insight and awareness.

Get it Right: Get Smart, Adapt and Overcome

Going around the Disaster-Improv loop several times is a learning experience. You learn that there is no such thing as failure, only feedback. You learn that perseverance is what gets you the ending to the story that you wanted. You learn that it is not about you and that you need to put other people first. You learn that the situation can often get worse before it gets better. There are plenty of unforeseen obstacles that can be used to justify quitting. After you go around a couple of times, it becomes less frightening. You discover that you really do get more than one chance to get it right. And that things getting worse does not mean you're doing it wrong. Keep trying. Think big. Look for learning. Rethink and try again.

Remember this:

"In the end, everything will be ok. If it's not ok, it's not yet the end."

Fernando Sabino
translated from Portuguese

Gap Analysis

*"Setting goals is the first step in
turning the invisible into the visible."*

Tony Robbins

Goals: Get Things Done or Get You Killed

There was a time in the world of business when
doing a Gap Analysis was the norm. The strategy goes
like this:

1. Understand your starting point (Point A)
2. Define your final goal (Point B)
3. Measure the gap between Point A and Point B
4. Figure out how to bridge the gap

It is straightforward and has some powerful
advantages. There is movement with this model. You
know where you are. You clearly know what this goal is.
You can mark your course and tell your team where you
are in terms of progress. It is a great way to get things
done. The only problem is that in a disaster it can get
you killed.

The Model

The 1D Gap Analysis

A ————————▶ B

The Wreck: Car Meets Truck

Imagine that you are driving across state with one of your best friends. As you come up over the hill you see an accident. It is a car against truck accident and the car is on fire. From a problem-solving perspective the goal is very clear: make sure that there is no one in the car and put the fire out.

Gap analysis perspective:

- Point A: the Car Is on Fire.
- Point B: the goal is for the car not to be on fire.

Pulling off to the side of the road you rapidly run through your options of how you are going to move from Point A to Point B. As you are jumping out of the car you yell to your friend to grab the fire extinguisher that is in the trunk. You run over to the car and luckily find that the driver has escaped. Your buddy starts to put the fire out with the fire extinguisher. Everything seems like it is moving along towards Point B very nicely.

And then you hear a noise.

You turn and look just in time to notice for the first time that the truck is a big white truck with red lettering on the side that says Propane. That is the last thing that you remember.

The Gap Analysis has a fatal flaw. It does not consider risk.

Get it Wrong: Increased Risk and Undiscovered Resources

Although this one dimensional view is helpful, it is fraught with danger because it does not consider risk. In the world of disaster medicine, we are trained to be situationally aware. When helping victims following a bombing, we are trained to have someone constantly looking out in all directions for danger lest the team become incapacitated by a second bomb or the propane tank that is burning and about to explode just behind us. Focusing only on the gap and trying to bridge it is noble but dangerous. If the medical team is taken out by a secondary blast not only is the team impacted, but those that we are trying to serve as well.

Without the Gap Analysis though, it is possible to remain stuck and not get anything done. It is easy to focus on the problem and feel defeated.

Get it Right: Movement

Although the Gap Analysis can be deadly if used in isolation, it certainly is essential for getting work done.

It defines direction, delineates the goal and precipitates movement. In fact, the Gap Analysis can be very powerful because of the Law of Target Fixation; the team will go where they look and the Gap Analysis points them in the right direction. It is useful to clarify and communicate the goals and objectives so that the team can be rallied and mobilized. Clearly, it is helpful to take a look at where we are starting from and where we want to end up. It just cannot be all there is. A one dimensional view is not enough.

SWOT Analysis

"The only thing worse than being blind is having sight but no vision."

Helen Keller

Take the Time to See

When the shortcomings of the one dimensional Gap Analysis became apparent, Albert Humphrey developed the concept of the SWOT Analysis. Considering Strengths, Weaknesses, Opportunities and Threats provides a more complete and certainly safer two dimensional view of the situation.

The SWOT analysis can be divided into two basic dimensions: risks and resources. Risks includes Weaknesses and Threats. Resources includes both Strengths and Opportunities.

The first reason to do a SWOT analysis is safety. While time is of the essence, safety remains crucial. Blindly sending assets into harm's way can be catastrophic. It is a rookie mistake to run into a situation without assessing the risk.

> Many years ago I was asked to be an observer for a county disaster drill that simulated a plane crash at the regional airport. The designers of the drill placed a school bus at one end of the runway. It was loaded with people that had moulage wounds and fake blood. They surrounded the bus with pans of oil and then lit the oil on fire. The bus was enveloped in thick black smoke. The director of the drill put out the call to begin the drill, "This is a drill, this is a drill, this is a drill. There has been a plane crash at the regional airport. All units respond. There has been a plane crash at the regional airport. All units respond." And then the action began!
>
> The fire department had pre-staged the trucks at the opposite end of the runway. I remember thinking before the drill began that this was an unfair test since they were already on site and they would be on the scene in seconds. With lights flashing and sirens blaring they came screaming down the runway. Stopwatches in hand, we watched as they responded. The shocking thing was that they didn't touch their first patient for a full 45 minutes! Hollywood would have gone nuts. However, the fire department was doing exactly what they had been trained to do. They set up a parameter, controlled the fire, put everything in place to begin triaging patients, re-assessed for safety and began to process the victims. To do otherwise could have resulted in ineffective chaos. Even worse, it could have put the entire team at risk.

The second reason for doing the SWOT analysis is to identify resources. Knowing the strengths of your team is exceedingly important. It is also important to know one's own strengths. This can be somewhat counterintuitive. Frequently, when people are under intense stress, they become very aware of their weaknesses and their faults. The disaster zone is not the time to work on improving one's weaknesses. It is a time to operate from strength. For example, one of my strengths is vision and inspiration. Managing the supply list is not. If I manage the supply list and the inventory, both the team and I will become frustrated. I know that it is much better for me to assign that task to someone who has that gift than it is for me to take it on myself. Of course, if there is no one available, as the leader I need to own that responsibility. Certainly, I can work on improving that area when I am not in a disaster zone. Do you know what your strengths are, or what the strengths of your team are? Use the free resource at www.dandiamondmd.com/viasurvey to find out. It is a tool that will give you and your team a list of your top five strengths. You may be surprised at your own results, and you may discover that some of your team members have strengths that you did not know about.

Discovering opportunities in the midst of a disaster can be somewhat like going on a scavenger hunt. I have found that I need to think both traditionally and improvisationally when I am working in the midst of these high-pressure environments. For example, we never really know where we are going to be working until we get there. Sometimes we are deployed to work in a hospital. Sometimes we are deployed to work out of a house. Sometimes we are deployed to work in a school, or perhaps a church. During Katrina we worked in a parking lot outside of the New Orleans Convention Center. We often have to scramble to find supplies. It is amazing how effective a cell phone camera can be when trying to explain to someone that speaks another language what it is that you are looking for.

Sometimes it is simple things that we are trying to fix. For example, as we were evacuating people from New Orleans, our wheelchairs kept disappearing. It turned out that people were taking them on the helicopters. Kicking ideas around, someone came up with a great solution. We had plenty of folding chairs that someone had brought us. We also had a bellman's cart with wheels on it. One of the evacuees "borrowed" it from a hotel to use it to haul their belongings. He was forced to leave it behind because it was too large to fit on a helicopter. We simply tied one of the folding chairs onto the bellman's cart and used it to ferry people out to the landing zone. Definitely not conventional but it solved the problem quite nicely. We start with the end goal in mind and then look for opportunities to adapt the resources in our environment to meet the need. It may not be pretty but we get the job done.

The Model

The 2D SWOT Analysis
RESOURCES

RISKS

Broken Buildings

In disasters we use a responsive organizational strategy called the Incident Command Structure (ICS). One of the top level roles in ICS is the Safety Officer. The job of the Safety Officer is to continuously survey the situation for potential threats. While everyone's eye immediately goes to the disaster, the Safety Officer is trained to look around in a full 360° lest the team be impacted by an unforeseen threat.

> When we were working in Haiti, we set up in a hospital that had been evacuated after the massive earthquake. I was able to locate an engineer that came and certified the building as safe to use. We moved in a set up rapidly. We had three operating tables going and we were busy! While we were

working to treat the wounded, one of the team members noticed that there was a large crack that had formed on the front of the building. About a third of the surgery suite was cantilevered out from the building. The crack ran right through the operating suite. We brought in some engineers and they had us build stone columns to support the front wall. If we hadn't had people looking, we could have lost the entire front of the suite!

For safety reasons it is always important to look all around you and not get seduced by what appears to be the main event. There is always the risk that something behind you or out of your field of view poses a threat to you, your team or your patients.

Combining Gap + SWOT = Vision + Action

The 1D+2D Analysis

RESOURCES

RISKS

Using either the Gap Analysis alone or the SWOT analysis alone is problematic. As we have seen, the Gap Analysis can be risky, if not downright life-threatening. The SWOT analysis, on the other hand, does not promote movement toward a goal. The SWOT analysis is important but it is all too possible to stay in analysis mode and never move forward. In disasters, we do not have time for that type of stalling. We cannot stay in analysis mode. We have to move forward. Therefore, combining the SWOT analysis and the Gap Analysis can be very helpful. Using the two together we can clearly see what the goal is and, using a 360° view of our risks and resources, move forward to accomplish the objective.

Gap + SWOT = Vision + Action

Get it Wrong: Derailed/Injured, Missed Opportunity

Without the SWOT Analysis, it is easy to be blindsided by unforeseen risks or miss the chance to make a difference by overlooking resources. It takes work to do the SWOT Analysis but it is well worth the effort. It does not happen automatically for most of us. It needs to be an intentional effort, and it needs to be something you practice. Without the Gap Analysis to accompany it, we can spend all day long in committee meetings and never get anything done.

Get it Right: Consider Risk/Resources

Combining the one-dimensional Gap Analysis and the two-dimensional SWOT Analysis gives us a wide-angle view of the situation and moves us along toward creating effective solutions to the challenges that we face. There is a good amount of "field wisdom" wrapped up in these two models, and we are beginning to move in the right direction. However, both a one-dimensional view and a two-dimensional view are no longer enough. As we have noted, resilience is no longer enough. It is not enough to just bounce back and survive. We want to thrive, and for that we need to consider a three-dimensional view.

GASP Analysis

"One of the greatest joys in my life is introducing two people, getting out of the way, and watching their relationship flourish."

Paul Bodnar

Introducing the GASP (Get A Spherical Perspective) Analysis

Consider your sphere of influence. Your sphere is a three-dimensional environment that is actually made up of many slices. Each of the slices is made up of a one-dimensional Gap Analysis and a two-dimensional SWOT Analysis. Depending on the situation, you can consider this sphere of influence to be made up of individuals on your team or departments within your organization. Each slice has its own problem set that they are trying to solve. Each set has its own strengths, weaknesses, opportunities and threats. Each of us brings a unique perspective. Each of us has a different sphere of influence.

The individual that will become the most valuable person in an organization is the one that can figure out how to match the resources of one slice with the needs of another slice.

And now we see how it all comes together. This relates directly to the discussion we had previously regarding engagement and mindset. If you're engaged in your work you will care about what happens to the people around you. If you have the Thriver Mindset, you approach your work believing that you have the power to make a difference and you do not care who gets the credit.

In order to impact the slices within your sphere of influence, it is necessary to take an interest and ask questions. As you consider the various slices within your sphere, ask people the following two questions:

1). What keeps you up at night?

2). What are you celebrating?

These two questions are great starting point for a conversation that will sometimes catch people by surprise. People are not used to having other people care about them on that level. When you take the time to find out what is keeping them up at night, you will have a good understanding of what problems are at the top of their mind. When you asked them what they are celebrating it will give you some insight into their recent victories and the resources that they have. Pay attention. Take mental notes. Look for opportunities to match the resources of one slice to the struggles of another. In so doing, you will become a conduit. Introduce them and get out of the way. It is a tremendously rewarding strategy. In the process, your entire sphere will become stronger.

On a side note, most people are also motivated by reciprocity. When one team does something to help another team, it is not long before the team that has been helped is offering their resources back to the other team. The whole sphere is changed and strengthened because you were engaged, cared enough to ask questions, believed you could make a difference and connected resources to needs.

The GASP Analysis

The 3D GASP Analysis

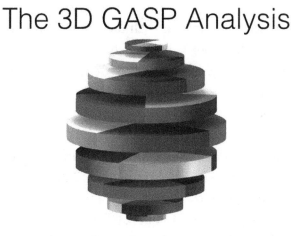

Get a Spherical Perspective

The Lab: Scientific Breakthrough!

A few years ago when I was pondering these concepts, I decided to take a stroll downstairs to the lab. I went down to ask them the simple question, "Are there two or three things that I could do differently to make your job better?" It was as if they didn't have to think about it. Actually, it was as if they may have already been talking about it before. They rattled off three things that I could do differently and I went back upstairs committed to trying to make their jobs better. A few weeks later, they came upstairs to visit me and asked the same question. I gave them a couple of things that I thought could make my job a bit better. My relationship with the lab is now stronger than ever. The junction between our two jurisdictions or slices has been strengthened.

If I choose the Thriver Mindset, my goal should be that I make the other team look like heroes. In so doing, the junction between our two departments becomes stronger. Who benefits? Ultimately the patient. But the organization benefits as well. My job satisfaction improved. The lab personnel felt like their job got better. It was not really even difficult to implement the changes that they requested. Simple questions. Taking the time to ask. A willingness to change. A commitment to putting other people first and a belief that you have the power to make a difference. These are the components that make for a very strong organization.

Get it Wrong: Silos Promote Impractical Solutions that Drain Enthusiasm and Stifle Innovation

Following Hurricane Katrina there were extensive investigations done regarding the levee system and why it failed. A preliminary report published by the University of California at Berkeley found that one of the places where the levees tended to fail was at the junction between two different jurisdictions. At these junctions the walls were found to have been made of different materials and even of different heights! The primary failure of the levees was from overtopping but the different wall heights focus the power of the water and cause the other side of the levee wall to undermine and then the entire section failed.

"The junction between two different jurisdictions should be the strongest point in the wall."

Dan Diamond, MD

This is similar to what happens in organizations. As health care organizations become more complex, the organizations frequently become more siloed as well. The weakest point in most organizations is the junction between two different jurisdictions. Each side points to the other and says, "That's not my job; that's their job!" When people and teams within organizations consider only their slice, the entire organization becomes weaker. When pressures rise there are shearing forces that occur at the junctions. In the worst-case scenario, patients lives can be at risk. There is also a significant impact on the efficiency, creativity, work satisfaction and the

101

reputation of the organization. The junction between two different jurisdictions should be the strongest point in the wall.

Get it Right: Movement + Risk/Resources + Spherical Approach = Transformational Impact

When we get this right, the impact can be transformational for an organization. Consider the common dilemma of a disparity between the upper level management and the front-line health care workers. It could start from either slice.

Someone from the upper-level management slice asks someone from the front-line slice, "What's keeping you up at night?" They learn from the front-line staff that one of the biggest problems that they have is a key problem with the order sets in their electronic medical record system. Perhaps that management person is aware of another hospital or system that has solved that problem and they are able to introduce the staff member to someone at the other facility so they can learn more. A new solution could be born from that process.

That is not an unusual scenario. It raises a bit more eyebrows when it goes in the other direction. But it can! What if someone from the frontline asks someone in upper management, "So, what's keeping you up at night?" They discover that the biggest struggle for management is trying to figure out how to decrease readmission rates for patients with congestive heart failure. The frontline staff member mentions that she was recently at a convention where she learned of an innovative new program that has been shown to decrease readmission rates. Eager to learn more, the two of them set up an appointment to go over her notes. A new program is born. Patients lives are improved and the bottom line for the organization is improved as well. These sorts of major breakthroughs happen when people consider their entire sphere of influence.

GASP Analysis. Get a Spherical Perspective.

Summary Part IV: Breaking Through Barriers when Times are Tough

"Success is stumbling from failure to failure with no loss of enthusiasm."

Winston Churchill

We have looked at the ingredients for problem solving under pressure. Using the underlying Law of Disaster-Improv, "There is no such thing as failure, only feedback", we move forward empowered to approach problem solving with a cyclical strategy. This allows us to continue trying until we reach an acceptable solution. It allows the use of divergent thinking as a starting point.

Divergent, emergent and convergent thinking are like seeing the world with a fish-eye lens, then horse blinders and then a magnifying glass. Remember that the natural tendency when one is discouraged is to see convergently — with a narrow field of view. If you want to discover new options, use humor and gratitude to expand your view like a divergent fish-eye lens. Look for new ways of doing things and combining ideas.

Emergent thinking is like putting the blinders on. It is a time to work with what you have. Look for opportunities to mix and match. Take a careful look at what you unearthed in the divergent phase. Count the costs. Consider the risks. Survey your resources from both the perspective of traditional implementation and improvisational implementation.

The convergent phase is like using a magnifying glass. It is a time for intense focus, planning and execution. Beware of getting stuck in the over analysis mode. Remember that Disaster-Improv is a cyclical strategy. The first pass does not have to be perfect. You will get another shot. The important strategy in the convergent phase is to focus and then move.

We work in a three dimensional world. Those that approach problem solving with a 3D view will become the most valuable to any organization. If you want to maximize your impact, combine the following three views:

- The 1D GAP Analysis: Define the starting point and clarify the goal.
- The 2D SWOT Analysis: Outline the resources (strengths + opportunities) and the risks (weaknesses + threats) so you can creatively bridge the gap and not get derailed in the process.
- The 3D GASP Analysis: Study the slices in your sphere of influence and discover opportunities to become a conduit between the risks and needs of one slice and the resources of another.

If you implement these strategies with a Thrivers Mindset, believing that you have the power to make a difference and you do not care who gets the credit, you will make a difference, leave a legacy and become one of the most valuable people in your sphere.

It is easy to ponder these things and agree that they make sense. But how do they actually work in the real world? How would you go about actually putting them into practice? Let me introduce you to Phedaline and her story, and we can watch these strategies unfold in the real world, under pressure and when it matters.

Phedaline's Story

Phedaline was only 13 years old when the earthquake brought Haiti to its knees. She was in their two room concrete house with her mother when the world began to shake. Bowls and cups shattered on the floor and the earthquake sounded like a massive train going through their house. Phedaline was horrified. Afraid that she was going to die she ran from the house but, in a terrible twist of fate, she was hit by a car as soon as she made it to the street. She was pinned under the car and the exhaust pipe seared the right side of her face and her right arm with second and third degree burns. The neighbors heard her screaming and several men ran over and actually lifted the car up and pulled her out. Covered with dirt and in agony from the burns, Phedaline was loaded into a car and taken to the United Nations compound because someone thought there would be medical help there.

I met Phedaline on day four. I had just arrived in Port-au-Prince. We were tasked with getting

King's Hospital back on line. It had been condemned as unsafe immediately after the earthquake. As part of my See phase, I went to the United Nations Field Hospital because that had been identified as the primary medical facility. I went there with the idea of gaining a greater understanding of their slice in my GASP analysis. I wanted to know what was going well and what was keeping them up at night. What I found was a medical team that had been up for four nights (and days)! I didn't have to ask, "What's keeping you up at night?" It was obvious. There were two tents. One tent had about 150 patients in it and the other tent close to 180. To make matters worse, the patients in the larger tent were the sicker ones. I have been doing disasters for more than 30 years but I have never seen as many broken and crushed people in my life. The destruction was devastating and, unfortunately, unforgettable.

It was clear what I could do to help. The doctors needed a break. I introduced myself to Dr. Hilarie Cranmer and told her about my previous disaster experience. She was the lead physician in the larger, sicker tent. She had been doing an absolutely amazing job but she was about to fall down from fatigue. What do you say to someone that has been giving so sacrificially without a care as to who gets the credit? How about "Want to take a nap?" I offered to take a shift so she could go find a place to sleep. She looked at me and with utter exhaustion said, "Really? You would do that for me?" "Of course, and when you come back I'll give it back to you. I'm not trying to take your place. I just want to give you a break." It was like giving a drink of water to a parched person dying in the desert.

During my shift, I met Phedaline. She was beautiful, but so broken. As a father of a teenage daughter, I couldn't help but care about her.

The next day we were able to open the doors at King's Hospital and start seeing patients. Knowing that the UN Field Hospital was overloaded and overwhelmed with patients, we drove a van over and asked if we could offload patients to King's. We had three orthopedic surgeons and operating rooms going constantly, so we were well equipped to deal with some of the orthopedic patients. As we went down the rows after rows of stretchers, the physicians at the UN assigned patients to us. When we got to Phedaline, they said, "How about her? Do you want to take Phedaline?" "Of course!" I blurted out. How could I not help her?

After we got back to King's I started thinking with my head and not my heart. I had a problem: a 13-year-old girl with severe facial and arm burns that clearly needed plastic surgery and skin grafts. OK, it was worse than that. I had three orthopedic surgeons that worked with hammers and saws. They wouldn't consider themselves the ideal sort to do technical plastic surgery on a little girl's face! Besides, we didn't have any of the equipment to do skin grafting. We needed a special instrument called a dermatome to remove a thin layer of skin from her leg to transplant to her face and arm.

Let's pause the story to look at where I stand:

Horizontal Engagement: Actively Engaged.

Vertical Tier: 1 (Purpose driven/Committed to overcome/Desire to leave a legacy)

See: It was quite a Gap. (And it was about to get worse.)

Gap + SWOT + GASP Analyses:

1) Point A: A 13-year-old girl with severe facial and arm burns
2) Strengths
   a) Pain medications
   b) Some antibiotics to prevent infection
   c) Clean dressings
   d) Loving staff
3) Weaknesses
   a) No plastic surgeon
   b) No dermatome
4) Opportunities
   a) Orthopedic surgeons doing delicate pediatric facial plastic surgery? **[Applied humor]**
   b) UN Field Hospital
   c) Israeli Hospital
   d) Incoming teams
   e) Evacuation
5) Threats
   a) Could not go out at night because of gang activity
   b) Infection
6) Other slices/teams
   a) UN:
      i) Needs: Offloading patients for them
      ii) Assets: Major supply depot that we can access
   b) Israeli needs:
      i) Needs: Trying to help them find an X-Ray bulb for their machine

       ii) Assets: Multi-specialty team, well organized and willing to partner.

   7) Point B: A healthy girl that needs facial plastic surgery so she will survive with only minimal scars and her family will know that they are loved.

Sort: Top priority was skin grafting to decrease infection and scarring risk.

Solve: Try the Israeli team to see if they had a plastic surgeon, or at least a dermatome.

I had an idea how to *Solve* this problem and thus established my first point of action. Back to the story:

> We headed over to the Israeli compound to see what we could find. To this day, I can still close my eyes and see Wilson, my driver, negotiate the roads covered with rubble, people and other vehicles. He drove like a famous Italian sports car driver. It took about 15 minutes before we were knocking on the big steel gate at the Israeli compound. The door slid open and we were met by a soldier with an Uzi machine gun. I had met the commandant earlier in the day and was trying to help him find an X-Ray bulb for their machine, so it wasn't very difficult to get by the guard. Unfortunately, as well organized as they were, they didn't have plastic surgery or a dermatome.

See: I still have the same Point A and Point B. The Israeli team cannot help. Gap unchanged. GASP improved (I now know more about their resources. They even have an ophthalmologist on their team.)

Sort: Still with the same priority.

Solve: Evacuation may be the best alternative

I figured that the best place to get her evacuated to the US for surgery was to find someone with a plane. The best place to find planes is at the airport. "Wilson, grab the car! We're heading to the airport." When we arrived at the airport we went straight to the command center. Imagine a 40ft shipping container on stilts that has been armor plated and then decorated with antennae all over the top. I knocked on the door and was greeted by an officer. After I explained the situation, he said that I needed to talk with Capt. Tippins and that she was located at the other end of the tarmac.

One of the best things about working in disasters is that you get to do things you normally would never get to do, because all of the rules are temporarily suspended. We just drove our car right down the tarmac! "Capt. Tippins, my name is Dr. Dan Diamond. I'm working at King's hospital and we have a 13-year-old girl that was pinned under a car and has severe burns of the face and arm. I need to get her evacuated to the US for facial plastic surgery. Can you help us?"

"Does she have a visa?" she replied.

I have to confess that it took everything within me to not say [**using my internal humor lens**], "No, but she has American Express!" A visa? How the heck were we going to get a visa for the United States? I asked Capt. Tippins for advice. She directed me to the US Embassy but told me to be sure to go to the "secret side door".

"By the way, Capt. Tippins, what's keeping you up at night?" I asked [**using my GASP Analysis**]. She said, "Oh man, we don't have anywhere to properly dispose of body parts and we are doing plenty of amputations."

"We can help with that. We have orthopedic surgeons that are doing much of the same and we have a burn pit. We'll take your parts." **[Using a GASP Analysis to link needs and resources between different slices of my sphere of influence.]**

"Really, you would do that for us?"

"Happy to help."

"Wilson, grab the car!"

When we arrived at the US Embassy, there were armed guards out front. I had my county ID with a bar code on it (the secret to access anywhere in the developing world is an ID with a bar code). We were allowed to park up front. I walked up to the guards and asked them how their day was going. Standing straight and with precision he answered, "Sir, we had one heck of a day! This morning we had to hold off 4,000 people at gunpoint". He whipped his machine gun into an action pose and then snapped back to attention.

"What did they want?" I replied.

"Visas!"

My heart sank. "Where is the secret side door?"

"Sir, there is no secret side door."

"Capt. Tippins from the US Air Force told me to be sure to go to the "secret side door" when I got here."

"Sir, there is no secret side door."

I didn't believe him so I carefully looked all around the building. I hate to admit it but, there is no secret side door. (Perhaps you need special goggles or something to see it.)

We met with the Nurse Practitioner that worked at the Embassy. "What do you want me to do? I can't help you get a visa."

See: My Gap just got bigger and my SWOT shows more Weaknesses.

1) Weaknesses:
   a) Time is running out
   b) Self-doubt: I am an idiot for taking her case. I was moved by emotion and should never have agreed to take her.
   c) Cannot get a visa
2) Point B
   a) A healthy girl that needs facial plastic surgery so she will have minimal scars and her family will know that they are loved.
   b) Need to evacuate
   c) Need a plane
   d) Need a visa

Wilson and I slowly walked back to the car, heartily discouraged. When we got home the Law of Disaster-Improv hit me right between the eyes: "There is no such thing as failure; only feedback." Failure or feedback? What was it going to be? If I considered this to be a "failure" then the whole process comes screeching to a halt. Game over. If I choose to look at it as "feedback" then we can go around the loop again with more information than we had before. After all, I'm definitely smarter now than I was the day before. The eventual outcome at this point was determined by one thing: my mindset. Did I still believe that I had the power to make a difference? Was I going to be a Giver or a Taker? Who was I serving? Myself or Phedaline?

I am going to pause at this point in the story to remind you that we were working long hard days. We were sleep deprived, sleeping on the floor in sleeping bags, in a different time zone, experiencing new customs, and still trying to figure each other out as a team since we had not worked together before. It would have been easy to become discouraged and quit. We had a long list of reasons that we could have used. I am sure you have a long list as well. Discouraged defeat would have been the default course to follow.

However, if you are going to follow the Disaster-Improv model, there is no room for failure. There is, however, plenty of room for mistakes because mistakes are only feedback.

Sort: Evacuation is still the best plan

Solve: Perhaps I need to try a different approach at the airport.

Continuing to remain engaged in the process, I kept trying to figure out another solution. No equipment, no facial plastic surgeon, no air-evacuation, no visa to get into the US. I decided to go back out to the airport and try a different approach with Capt. Tippins. "Wilson, grab the car. We're heading back to the airport."

Capt. Tippins was busy at work at the far end of the runway. I asked her if I might have just three minutes of her time.

"Capt. Tippins, I would like you to imagine that you and I are standing in your front yard and it is a nice sunny day. None of this is here. There are no helicopters, no jets, no M.A.S.H unit, no crates of supplies. It's just you and me. The grass is green beneath our feet. Can you see it? Now, imagine that this is your daughter." Then I showed her the photo of Phedaline.

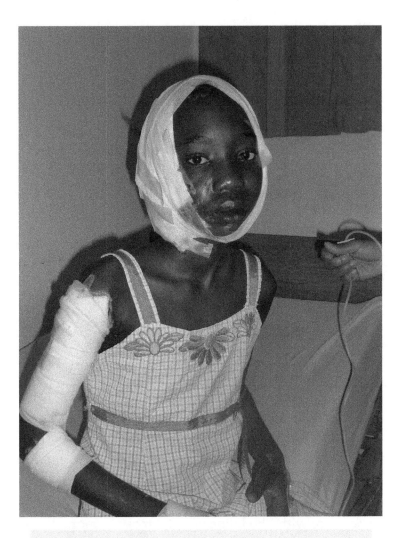

It stopped Capt. Tippins in her tracks. "Oh" followed by a long pause, "you need to talk to my boss". She pointed across the clearing.

I decided to cut to the chase. I said the same thing to him. "Imagine that none of this is here and we are standing in your front yard...." He looked at me eye-to-eye, soul-to-soul as his world came to a screeching halt. "Let me see what I can do. How do I get a hold of you?"

Wilson and I headed back to our compound with renewed hope that we might actually get help for Phedaline. Less than 45 minutes later my cell phone rang. Capt. Tippins was so excited the words came out at double speed, "If you can get Phedaline here in 45 minutes, we can get her evacuated to the US today!"

"Wilson, get the car!"

Phedaline was evacuated later that day to Miami and then transported to the Miami Children's Hospital where she underwent a series of surgeries to treat her burns.

She made it. Gap closed. Relationships strengthened. Sphere improved. Multiple lives impacted.

Strategies:

- Divergent-Emergent-Convergent Thinking
- Disaster-Improv: No failure; only feedback.
- Gap + SWOT + GASP

These are trench tested concepts that work even in the worst of circumstances. When I talked with Capt. Tippins after the event, she shared with me that her experience with Phedaline was the most memorable and meaningful encounter of the entire Haitian disaster experience. It certainly was mine as well.

Creating Lasting Change

Delivering world class health care in the midst of these times of tremendous change requires an effective mindset, increasing engagement and improvisational problem solving skills. Those that make the greatest positive impact will do the work to understand their sphere of influence and look for opportunities to become a conduit between the slices of their sphere. The Thriver Mindset of empowered giving makes this possible.

Some people will undoubtedly be paralyzed by fear, become discouraged and get stuck thinking only convergently. They will focus on the problems and miss the opportunities to have game changing novel approaches to deliver great care in new and innovative ways. Others will stay engaged and change the world around them by putting others first, and by thinking divergently *then* emergently *then* convergently. They will break through barriers and empower others by not caring who gets the credit.

These concepts are true from the board room to the operating room, from the clinic to the business office; and from the nurse's aid to the neurosurgeon. When we become engaged, believe that we can make a difference and put others first we will become, like the thrivers of major disasters, unstoppable.

So what are you going to do now? How is the information in the book going to make a lasting change? It really comes down to a series of daily choices for you and your team:

- Which way am I facing? Am I looking at what's wrong, or where I want to end up? Remember, you go where you look!
- How can I become more engaged and leave a legacy?
- Since no one can take away my right to choose, will I choose to be powerless or powerful?
- What is my purpose? Will I be a taker or a giver?
- When I seem to be stuck solving a problem, am I using divergent thinking, emergent thinking or convergent thinking?
- Where are we trying to go? What is our Point B?
- What are our risks and resources (SWOT)?
- How can I positively impact my sphere of influence?
  - Will I take the time to ask other people and teams, "So, what's keeping you up at night?"
  - Will I take an interest and ask other people and teams, "What are you and your team celebrating?"
  - Will I take a risk and ask, "What can I do differently to make your job easier or better?"
- Do I care who gets the credit?
- What can I do to make the people and teams around me into heroes?

These are indeed times of tremendous change. They are stressful and they can be exhausting. These are also times of opportunity for those that stay engaged and press on to make a difference. After the super typhoon

118

hit the Philippines, my friend Mayor Romualdez asked his team, "So what do you want to do? Are you going to sit this one out? Your grandchildren are going to ask you, 'What did you do?'"

What will *you* tell them?

Appendix/Models

Face Success: You Go Where You Look

Face Success: You Go Where You Look

External Impact

Builds Division	Drains Energy	Slows Creativity	Builds Loyalty
Sabotages Efforts	Does Not Finish	Needs Direction	Adapts to Change
Discourages Team	Frustrates Team	Stifles Teamwork	Motivates Team
ACTIVELY DISENGAGED!	**PASSIVELY DISCONNECTED**	**PASSIVELY CONNECTED**	**ACTIVELY ENGAGED!**
Self-Focused	Pessimistic	Follower	Owner
Anger	Helpless	Task Focused	Solutions Focused
Catastrophic RXN	Irrelevant Tasks	Unaware	Big Picture

Internal Impact

Performance Tiers

Performance Tiers

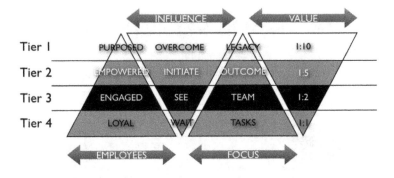

The Thriver Matrix

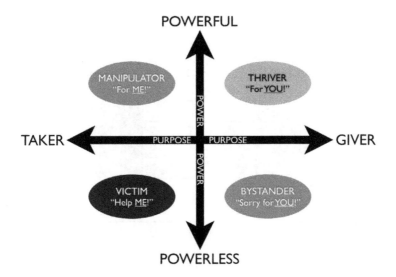

Thinking Strategies

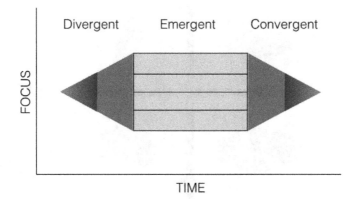

Adapted from Dave Gray and Sunni Brown and James Macanufo, *Gamestorming: A Playbook for Innovators, Rulebreakers, and Changemakers* [Kindle Edition]. loc. 894

Gap Analysis

The 1D Gap Analysis

A ⟶ B

SWOT Analysis

The 2D SWOT Analysis

RESOURCES

RISKS

Combined Gap + SWOT Analysis

The 1D+2D Analysis

RESOURCES

RISKS

GASP Analysis

The 3D GASP Analysis

Get a Spherical Perspective

Disaster-Improv

Acknowledgements

My wife, Debbie, is amazing. Despite the fact that she has faced tremendous obstacles with her health, she has stayed enthusiastically engaged. When I have had doubts about my work, she is quick to respond with a strong dose of encouragement. Debbie has been very supportive of my passion to "make a dent on the world". Thank you for the companionship. "Two are better than one because they have a good return for their labor." Ecclesiastes 4:9

Paul, Josh and Sarah, my three grown children, are fantastic. Their excitement about this project has fueled my passion when I have been burning the midnight oil. Thanks for your humor, feedback and friendship. I am proud to be your Dad.

I am not too old to thank my Mom, Barbara. She is an inspiration to many and she taught me how to be persistent. I can still hear the advice that she gave me in High School as I struggled with homework from time to time: "Just keep going and do the best that you can." Thanks for seeing me through the challenges.

A guy could not ask for better buddies than Chris Clark, Greg Meadows, Paul Wright and Dr. Bob Rankin. Thank you for being such a great, albeit informal, Board of Directors. I appreciate the insights that each of you have brought to this project and to my life. My relationships with each of you have been tremendously rewarding and shaped me into the man I have become. I am a better husband, father, physician and friend because of you guys. "As iron sharpens iron, so one person sharpens another." Proverbs 27:17.

This truly has been an international effort. Carolyn "Yen" Remitar has been a wonderful personal assistant. Her hard work and research helped to fill in the gaps. I am proud to have a partner that works from the Philippines. I appreciate your commitment, resilience and patience. Yen, thank you for saying "yes" when I asked you to join my team.

I have enjoyed working with the fabulous Australian editor, Michelle Phillips. She has a great mind, outstanding insights and she has been an absolute joy to work with. When I was struggling for words, she helped me break through the barriers. I am so grateful for her willingness to walk me through this process. Peter Cook was right when he said that she was perfect for the job.

With her wonderful "teacher's eye", Rita Eklund helped me produce a book with proper grammar and spelling thus making this book much easier to read.

I am exceedingly grateful for the mentorship that I have received from Matt Church and Peter Cook of the Thought Leaders Business School in Australia. They taught me how to develop, grow and mature my thoughts and ideas. If you have found this book to be at all helpful, it is due to the investment that Matt and Peter have made to bring about my growth as a thought leader. Without their systems and strategies, these ideas would still be floating around in my head.

ABOUT THE AUTHOR

Dr. Diamond works with organizations around the globe that want to equip their people to perform under pressure. For information on how Dr. Diamond can serve your organization, please visit

www.dandiamondmd.com

Dr. Diamond founded and serves as the Director of the Nation's first state-affiliated medical disaster response team and he has responded to a variety of international disasters. Following Hurricane Katrina, he played a strategic role as Director of the Mass Casualty Triage Unit at the New Orleans Convention Center. He has been interviewed on CNN, Larry King Live and Anderson Cooper. He is a member of the National Speakers Association and the Past-President of NSA Northwest.

As an experienced family physician and an award-winning educator, Dr. Diamond delivers practical information with creativity and skill. Participants experience learning through a variety of effective strategies that foster rapid mastery of new information. Well known for creating an exciting learning environment, Dr. Diamond engages the mind of the learner leaving participants with an experience and information they will never forget.

After earning his medical degree from University of Washington, Dr. Diamond completed his residency in Family Medicine in Milwaukee, WI. The American Academy of Family Physicians awarded Dr. Diamond the degree of Fellow and he is Board Certified with the American Board of Family Physicians. Dr. Diamond is a Clinical Assistant Professor at the University of Washington School of Medicine.

In 2010, the American Red Cross gave him the "Real Hero" award and he also received the Washington Sate Governor's Award of Excellence for his work in Haiti. In 2014, Dr. Diamond received the President's Volunteer Service Award from President Obama and he also received the Quality of Care Lifetime Achievement Award, Healthcare Heroes.

Dr. Diamond and his wife Debbie enjoy their three children: Paul, Josh and Sarah. The Diamond family is big on traditions, humor and love.

For more more information:

Email: events@dandiamondmd.com
Website: www.dandiamondmd.com.
Blog: www.dandiamondmd.com/blog
Twitter: @dandiamondmd